So Why Do I Need
A CHURCH?

So Why Do I Need
A CHURCH?

Other than nurturing a daily walk with God through personal Bible study and prayer, nothing is more important in the life of a Christian than being actively involved in a local church. As you read this book you will discover why.

CLAYTON DOUGAN

SO WHY DO I NEED A CHURCH
By: Clayton Dougan
Copyright © 2012
GOSPEL FOLIO PRESS
All Rights Reserved

Published by
GOSPEL FOLIO PRESS
304 Killaly St. W.
Port Colborne, ON L3K 6A6
CANADA

ISBN:9781926765853

Cover design by Rachel VandenBerg and Danielle Elzinga

All Scripture quotations from the
King James Version unless otherwise noted.

Printed in USA

Table Of Contents

SECTION 1

I Need A Church
Because I need to be part of a praying community
(1 Peter 4:7)

SECTION 2

I Need A Church
Because I need to learn how to love fervently and to be loved
(1 Peter 4:8-9)

SECTION 3

I Need A Church
Because it is where God can make me most effective in making a difference (1 Peter 4:10)

SECTION 4

I Need A Church
Because I need to be highly motivated
(1 Peter 4:11)

Dedication

This book is gratefully dedicated to the memory of a past generation of church elders at Maddiston Evangelical Church in Scotland. Their godly influence remains with me to this day.

This book is also gratefully dedicated to the memory of a past generation of elders and to the present generation of elders at Olivet Evangelical Church, Falkirk, Scotland. Their prayerful care has been and is an enormous source of encouragement.

Acknowledgements

I wish, first of all, to gratefully acknowledge the constant support and encouragement I have received from my wife Isobel.

Our board of directors at Evangelism International, Louise Parton, Al Kelly, Bert Boyd, Cathy Sakiyama, Garry Sedun and Steve Foster have never wavered in their encouragement either. They have helped so much in giving valuable advice and also in certain business aspects of the writing process. Their prayerful support is also deeply valued.

Jane Ryder has done me the great service of reviewing the manuscript and making many valuable suggestions as to how the message of this book could be more effectively presented.

Rob and Irene Flett made it possible for me to have a week of quiet, prayerful reflection to review the manuscript in final preparation for publishing. For this I will be for ever grateful.

Andy and Anita Stewart are warmly thanked for their great kindness in vastly improving my computer equipment. This has meant I have had so many more resources literally at my fingertips.

Introduction

Next only to biblical illiteracy, church hopping has to be the saddest malaise in today's church. And it is safe to say there is a direct link between the two.

As one who has great cause to be profoundly grateful for my church background I feel I am able to write with some conviction as to why answering the question posed by the title of this book is so vitally important. The first church I every belonged to experienced a radical transition from mediocrity to functioning with the glory of God among us. The change came through a time of genuine revival. Everything was soaked in prayer, God's love could be felt among the people. This was the result of the healing of wounds caused by divisiveness. There was a great deal of true repentance and genuine reconciliation. The church was known for the warmth of its hospitality among the members and in the wider community. We were all encouraged to identify and develop our God given gifts thus contributing to the health and growth of the church. All this was greatly helped because the leadership saw to it that we were constantly being built up in our faith through a high standard of Bible teaching from teachers who had a high view of scripture. The name of the Lord was truly being glorified. It was not uncommon for elders and others to be in tears in prayer meetings as they prayed over lost people in the local community. Many of those prayed for came to faith in Christ and gave expression to their new found life by being baptized and going on to live consistent, godly lives.

Therefore it may seem obvious but the first question to be asked ought to be, what kind of church do I need? Answer; I need a church that is functioning properly. There are many churches priding themselves in being doctrinally correct yet they are not functioning as they ought. The sad situation in many is as it was in Israel just prior to God raising up the Prophet Samuel, the last of the Judges; the glory of God had departed from among His people because the ark of God, the symbol of God's presence, had been captured. Israel's enemies had reason to gloat because, in their minds, they had been victorious over Israel's God (1 Sam. 4). What could be described as a kind of "Post Modern" mind set was the order of the day, *"...everyone did what was right in his own eyes"* (Judg. 21:25). The people were not hearing from God, mainly because they were so spiritually bankrupt they **could not** hear from God. *"Word from the Lord was rare in those days, visions were infrequent"* (1 Sam. 3:1).

Our 21st century western Church gives the outside world so much cause to gloat. Because there is so little God consciousness among us who profess to be God's people, there is little God consciousness in society as a whole. In other words the glory of God has departed. The secular humanistic world is having a field day. Their hand is strengthened by the weakness and ineffectiveness of the very people who profess to know God who is all powerful, all knowing and "always present everywhere."[1] The very people who talk about serving a risen Saviour show very little evidence of His resurrection life in their personal lives, their families, their work place and their churches.

Stemming from the number one malaise in the wider Christian community these days, that of not reading and studying God's word (see my first book, *So Why Do I Need The Bible?*), is the consequent sickness of so many not being truly planted in a local church. Church hopping is the norm. People are constantly on the move attending the church which happens to be the flavor of the month; the church with the new pastor, good music, an active youth program and teaching which often does little more than tickle the ears.

The reasons professing Christians have given me for not attending a local church regularly are legion. Some are not reasons at all but, in the light of the biblical picture of what

---

1   J. I. Packer, *New Dictionary of Theology*, IVP 1988.

it means to be *"grow*[ing] *in grace"* (2 Pet. 3:18), are merely
feeble excuses. Others have reasons which are serious. Yet,
even with some of those, if the individuals are growing in the
knowledge of God they will learn to deal with the problems in
a biblical fashion. Regarding the more serious reasons, suffice
it to say it is not always the fault of the people in the congregation. A spirit of control and manipulation in areas of church
leadership can be so damaging. Pastoral visiting of congregation members in their own homes is woefully inadequate. As
a result those in leadership do not know whether or not the
sheep are really being fed. In other situations there is no vision
and, as a result, no real leadership at all. I could go on. For
over four decades as a traveling evangelist and Bible teacher
I have done a great deal of pastoral work with churches of
varying denominations. Sometimes it has been for a year or
two years at a time and sometimes for a few months or weeks.
This has enabled me to observe the problem both closely and
in a more detached way.

Being convinced of God's call to write this book, it is my
intention to base all that follows on what I believe to be the
core section in 1st Peter namely chapter 4 verses 7 - 11. It seems
to me that what ought to be the core values of any church are
clearly set out in those verses.

It is important to keep in mind the background to this
New Testament letter. As is the case with much of the New
Testament it was written to Christians who were scattered. In
the case of those to whom Peter was writing they were scattered over "the various parts of Asia Minor north of the Taurus
Mountains...So they were called 'sojourners', a word which
emphasizes both alien nationality and temporary residence
(see also 1 Pet. 1:17)"[2] They were scattered because they lived
constantly with persecution.

The challenge therefore is to function in spite of and not
because of the current political, cultural and social conditions
around us. While constitution and form, based on God's word,
are important, they are dead if not accompanied by radical

---

2   A. M. Stibbs and A. F. Wallis, *1 Peter: Tyndale N.T. Commentaries*, IVP 1983

holiness in the body of believers leading to effective contact with the community at large.

Sometimes I wonder about the kind of advice, which I must confess I have given from time to time, which encourages a person to "shop around" when wondering which church to become part of. The trouble with such advice is it pampers to the mind set, what does a particular church have to offer me? Does it meet my needs? The more mature attitude ought rather to be, what do I have to offer that church to contribute to its health and growth? Answering the latter question is the real way to ensure your own growth and well being in your walk with God. To say that you have nothing to offer a church is simply not true. If you know Christ as your Saviour, you are a member of His body of which He is the head, therefore His life is in you. This means that, just as a member of your own physical body has its own unique function, so you, as a member of Christ's body, are uniquely gifted to function for the glory of God as directed by the head.

Another aspect of the malaise we are dealing with in this book is simply opting out of church all together. Such an attitude is, I believe, a huge mistake. Were you ever to have the unfortunate experience of having a limb amputated, it would never enter your head to return to the hospital to ask after the welfare of your amputated arm or leg. You would never even think of that old part of you functioning as it once did when healthy and part of your body. Such a situation is absurd. All illustrations have their limitations I know but thinking you can function as a healthy member of Christ's body while keeping yourself detached from it is just as absurd. While it is true that knowing Christ as personal Saviour means you are eternally secure in Him, you will not be in a truly healthy spiritual condition keeping yourself detached from active fellowship with God's people. You are putting yourself in a very dangerous position, opening yourself up to all kinds of attacks from the devil. There is also the added tragedy of your God given gifting, that which was given to you the moment you were born again, lying dormant instead of contributing to the life and growth of what ought to be your local church.

A reading of the New Testament makes it very clear that God's way of working in the world in the run up to the coming of Christ is through the local church. While it is thrilling to be part of the church worldwide it is also imperative to remember that local churches in communities all over the world exist to give expression to the life of Christ. This is what makes the church so unique. The church, Christ's body, is people called out of the world, placed, by God Himself *"in Christ"* (1 Cor. 1:30; 2 Cor. 1:21-22). Christ as the very life of that body, living on the inside of every member, gives expression to His life through each member (Rom. 12:4-6; 1 Cor. 12:12-21). It is also very important to understand that no Christian in limbo can even begin to comprehend *"what is the breadth and length and height and depth, and to know the love of Christ which surpasses knowledge"*; only *"with all the saints."* That is because the plan of God is, *"that you may be filled up to all the fulness of God"* (Eph. 3:17-19). All utterly impossible in isolation.

My prayer for this book therefore is that it will help you, the reader, to become firmly and selflessly planted in a church in your community. It must be a church which has a vision to uncompromisingly teach God's word so as to build up its members in their faith. It also needs to be one which builds bridges to the local community with a view of seeing lost people coming to faith in Christ. All this for the glory of God.

Before moving on it must be said that if a new church is to be planted it must have in place all that will nurture the new plant. By that I mean mature and gifted leaders who will teach God's word and give godly leadership. They will have vision to make a difference in the surrounding community and not just be another house Bible study. I know there were house churches in New Testament times (Phil. 2) but they can hardly be compared with today's house churches. See www.vision-ministries.org

SECTION 1

I Need A Church

Because I need to be part of a praying community
1 Peter 4:7

Something to think about...

The idea that you can survive and grow as a Christian without being part of the fellowship of a local church is simply untrue (see the introduction to this book). May I encourage you to decide to be very prayerful about the church in which the Lord wants you to be planted. If you are already planted in a church may I encourage you to *"devote yourself to prayer"* on behalf of that part of Christ's body (Rom. 12:9-13). Every Christian needs to be part of a praying church.

ONE

Praying with the Big Picture in View

Were we to experience persecution would we be more vibrant in our walk with the Lord Jesus? On the other hand, were we to be more vibrant in our walk with Him, would we experience persecution? The latter is much more likely to be true. Remember, Jesus spoke of the world hating His followers because it hated Him first (see John 15:18-20). Again Jesus said, *"...in the world you have tribulation, but take courage I have overcome the world"* (John 16:33). In 2004 I had the huge privilege of spending several weeks with seriously persecuted disciples of Jesus in southern Sudan. Between the years 1983 and 2004 literally millions of people had been killed. A large number of them because they refused to renounce their faith in Christ. The Lord Jesus was so real to them and their relationship with Him so vibrant that they would rather die than deny their Saviour. What does that have to do with me and the church to which I belong I hear you ask? Simply this; it was against such a background of persecution that the Apostle Peter wrote his first letter. His concern was for God's people of his day to function as a healthy expression of the life of Christ within them, and all for the spiritual health and well being of one another. Even in our western nations the possibility of persecution looms larger all the time. The encouraging and upbuilding vibrancy of a healthy church helps prepare us for whatever testing lies ahead. Many of the first century church were used as scapegoats for the fire of Rome. Others were looked upon as social misfits. Perhaps this is what is in Peter's mind when he writes 1 Peter 4:14; *"if you are reviled for the name of Christ you are blessed, because the Spirit of glory and of God rests on you."*

Before going any further it is important to note that, while this book is concerned mainly with belonging to a particular church in the community where you live, we must not lose sight of the whole body of Christ which is the church made up of people from every nation on earth. Such people are those who have identified themselves with the Lord Jesus Christ as their personal Saviour and Lord and, as a result, are experiencing His resurrection life within them. It is therefore important to see that, in spite of all the sad divisions in the church, *"There is one body..."* (Eph. 4:4). All believers in the Lord Jesus are *"by one Spirit...baptized into one body"* (1 Cor. 10:12). Dr. John Stott, in his commentary on Ephesians 4:3-6, helpfully distinguishes between *"the visible church"* and *"the invisible church."* Dr. Stott points out that because there is *"one body and one Spirit...and one God and Father..."* there can only be one Christian body. He calls this "the invisible church, whose members are known only to God." The sad "disunity", he makes clear, is seen in what he calls "the visible church." Therefore the challenge today with regard to the church's unity is to so "walk in a manner worthy of the calling with which you have been called" so as to "maintain" that unity.[3]

It is essential to emphasize that, as believers in the Lord Jesus, we are called out of the world to be identified with Him not only as Saviour but as Lord. In other words to be part of His body; to be His bride. Biblical pictures of the church are very telling. The church is called Christ's body of which He is the head, (Eph. 1:22-23). In a body every member is important and has a unique function to fulfill. Years ago I broke my right wrist and being right handed I soon realized how complicated life could become when the left hand was trying to do what the right hand was supposed to be doing. Our bodies function as they ought when each member is fulfilling the role for which it was designed, all the time taking directions from the head. It is Christ's life which is flowing through each member of His body. After all being a real Christian means having "eternal life" which is His life. The Apostle John tells us, "...

---

3   John R. W. Stott, *God's New Society: The Message of Ephesians*, IVP, 1979, pages 150 - 155

that God has given us eternal life and this life is in His Son. He who has the Son has the life; he who does not have the Son of God does not have the life" (1 John 5:11-12). When a person truly repents of sin and trusts Christ as Saviour and Lord, the life transformation is so radical that such a person is described as being "a new creature" so much so that, *"old things have passed away... new things have come"* (2 Cor. 5:17).

Another biblical picture is of the church as the Bride of Christ. The bride is pictured in Ephesians 5 as being Christ's own for whom He gave Himself, whom He wants to sanctify, or set apart for Himself. We are told that one day He will *"present to Himself the church in all her glory"* (Eph. 5:22-32). While walking the other day in one of our beautiful parks in the city of Victoria, B.C., my wife and I came on a bridal party having photographs taken. It was so easy to identify the bride from everyone else in the wedding party and from all the people enjoying the park that day. She stood out because of the beauty of who she was and of what she was wearing. She was not ashamed of being a bride. In fact she reveled in the fact that all visiting the park that day could share her joy. She was the expression of a new life begun, filled with all kinds of hope for the future. There was a certain glory about that young woman which had the effect of drawing observers into the bridal party. I could not help thinking what a picture she was of what the church ought to be in the world. If the glory of Christ were really upon us; if we have seen *"the light of the knowledge of the glory of God in the face of Jesus Christ"* (2 Cor. 4:6), people in our communities would stop and take notice. They would never be able to pass by unaffected. In many cases they would be drawn to us realizing we have something they do not have. We would be in stark contrast to the world in which most people live; a world that has lost its way and is without hope. That young bride in the park was glowing. There was a radiance about her. It was that, as much as what she was wearing which drew our attention to her.

I was with a group of Christians recently to preach in their church. Towards the close of the communion service one of the congregation shared part of his story. By the glow on his face I could tell that remembering Christ's death by taking bread and wine, symbols of the Lord's broken body and poured out blood, this man's heart was moved all over again. He told us how back in the 1970's his heart was so hard against God and the church. He was well educated and an agnostic. Through a visiting evangelist he learned that God loved him, and that Christ died for him so he could experience complete forgiveness and receive new life from Christ. His heart was hard and his life was empty and falling apart. As the Holy Spirit continued to work on him the hard heart melted, he handed himself over to Christ and the empty, broken life was filled with God's gift of eternal life and put together again as he became a *"new creature"* in Christ (2 Cor. 5:17). Although this happened many years ago; by the glow in his face and the obvious emotion in his voice, I could tell it was all as fresh and new as though it only happened yesterday. Remembering the death of Christ in that communion service caused this good man to rejoice in all God had done in his life, and in the hope filling his heart for the future. The glory of God was upon him.

In a real sense there was a certain other worldliness about the bride in the park and the congregation member at the communion service. Both were demonstrating where their focus was. For the bride, her focus was the bridegroom. Her face lit up at the very sight of him. For the one remembering all the Lord Jesus had done for him, his focus, as one who had become part of the Bride of Christ, was Christ Himself, the bridegroom of the Church. All this beautifully illustrates how belonging to the Body and Bride of Christ means being called out of this world. It does not take much imagination to see that the world we live in is very broken. Today's world system is built on greed, selfishness, lust and pride (see 1 John 2:16). Being part of Christ's Body and Bride means being able to live in this present broken world but, at the same time, being able to enjoy the life and glory of the world to come. The Christian's focus is on the Lord Jesus who has healed the brokenness in his or her life, and by so doing, has enabled that person to live in freedom from the sin which previously was the cause of all the brokenness. This is possible because the Christian has Christ, by the Holy Spirit, living on the inside of him or her. Such a life is now lived, not for this world but for *"Christ in* [them] *the hope of glory"* (Col. 1:27). It is worth mentioning that while environmentally the present world is still a beautiful place, it is not as beautiful as it was when originally created, (see Rom. 8:18-22) nor as the new heaven and the new earth will be one day (see Rev. 21:1). So the idea of being called out of this world is never meant to be seen negatively but rather, as it is, very freeing and full of hope.

First century Christians were totally focussed on the historic resurrection of Christ from the dead. The coming of the Holy Spirit into the world and, as a result of their faith in Christ, into their individual lives, transformed them. As a result they were so filled with hope that they were willing to suffer and even to die for Christ. This is why the Apostle Peter spends so much time encouraging them in their suffering telling them their suffering represented a time of testing (1 Pet. 4:12). He described their experience as being *"reviled for the name of Christ"* adding that when this happens they *"are blessed because the Spirit and glory of Christ rests on you."* If you read the whole of 1 Peter chapter four you will see clearly that, whether first century Christians or 21st century ones, the life transformation is so radical and the resulting hope so certain they are willing to suffer to the extent of laying down their lives for "the name", Christ. It beats suffering as an "evildoer" any day. It may look as though judgement were coming upon the believers in Jesus, but such "judgement" is nothing compared to that which is coming on *"those who do not obey the gospel of our Lord Jesus Christ"* (2 Thess. 1:8). Having had the privilege of spending time with 21st century believers in Jesus who are suffering terrible atrocities for "the name" of Christ I have seen, first hand, that their suffering is real and yet their joy is full of the glory of God. Listen to the words of Jesus Himself, *"Blessed are you when people insult you and persecute you, and falsely say all kinds of evil against you because of Me. Rejoice and be glad, for your reward in heaven is great…"* (Matt. 5:11-12).

This is what Jesus meant when He talked to His disciples about letting their light shine before men (Matt. 5:16). By so doing they were allowing the glory of God to shine from their lives. Someone once said, "the darker it becomes, the better you can see the stars." When with those African Christians mentioned above, I recall lying on the ground one night gazing up at the African sky. Because our team was a long way from the nearest city there was a total absence of the lights of our broken world. The sky was dark and clear and, as a result the stars seemed to shine with added glory. It made a truly awesome sight in the blackness of the African sky.

The godless world around us is pretty dark. There are so many hurting and broken lives. Present day Christians need to wake up to the fact that we are part of the amazing plan of God for the ages. We are part of what Peter calls, *"the end of all things"* (1 Pet. 4:7). These are the times described graphically by Paul as *"the last days"* (2 Tim. 3:1); days when people are, *"lovers of self, lovers of money, boastful, arrogant, revilers, disobedient to parents, ungrateful, unholy, unloving, irreconcilable, malicious gossips, without self-control, brutal, haters of good, treacherous, reckless, conceited, lovers of pleasure rather than lovers of God, holding a form of godliness, although they have denied its power"* (2 Tim. 3:2-5). Hebrews 1:2-3 tells us that when Jesus Christ, the Son of God, came into the world He was God's last word to humanity. His coming inaugurated the "last days" or "the end of all things." Proof of this lies in the historical reality of Christ's substitutionary death on the cross (*"when He had made purification of sins"*), and on His bodily resurrection and ascension to Heaven (*"He sat down at the right hand of the Majesty on high"*). When Paul the Apostle preached the gospel in Thessalonica the message had a radical effect. People there *"turned to God from idols to serve the living and true God, and to wait for His Son from Heaven, whom He raised from the dead, that is Jesus, who rescues us from the wrath to come"* (1 Thess. 1:9-10). While we have no idea when the Lord Jesus will return we know it could be at any moment. Peter is not attempting to be a sensationalist when he says, *"the end of all things is near."* He means what he says. His words are meant to be a wake up call to all who claim to know Christ as Saviour. Life ought to be lived in the realization that these are the last days; Christ is coming again. How can we believe that and not make it a priority to be in a constant state of readiness? If Christ's return to take us home to Heaven were anything other than imminent, there would be little point to Peter's statement.

Without being melodramatic; rather, I trust, realistic, we must face the fact that the end of our individual lives could happen at any time even as we wait for the coming of the Lord. Dr. Barnes has said, when commenting on 1 Peter 4:7 and the end of life, "it fixes our character, it seals our destiny, it makes all… unchangeable."[4] In a small cemetery near Victoria, B.C. there is a grave stone on which are engraved the words, "we are in memory what we were in life." I recall standing looking at that grave for quite some time and sensing all over again how short life really is. If I knew the Lord were returning today or that my life was to end today would there be changes I would want to make in my present life style? I will have more to say about the coming of the Lord in a later chapter, but for now may I remind you that this is one of the non-negotiable truths of our faith as Christians; Jesus is coming again. Now I am aware there are various view points as to events surrounding the coming of the Lord and I respect that. However one tragic result of there being so many points of view is that we very rarely hear the second coming of Christ preached in our churches these days. This is a foundational doctrine of our faith and one which, if preached with boldness, will stimulate an awareness of eternity and challenge us all to holy living.

It is little wonder the prayer ministry in most churches is so pathetic when, by and large we have lost the sense of the big picture of which we are part. We live our lives in time which is a tiny blip when compared with the awesomeness of eternity. We are all moving towards eternity therefore the need of the hour is to never lose sight of that and answer the question posed by this book always with the big picture in view.

Challenge

Take time today, in the quietness of God's presence, to allow Peter's words to sink in, *the end of all things is near; therefore…"* (1 Pet. 4:7).

---

4   Albert Barnes; *Barnes' Notes on the New Testament*

TWO

Keeping a Clear Mind

Whatever challenge Peter had in mind it is high time for all of us to, *"awaken from sleep; for now our salvation is nearer than when we believed"* (Rom. 13:11). This is not the time for complacency or mediocrity. This is the time for *"sound judgement and a sober spirit,"* or, as the New International Version puts it, it is a time to *"be clear minded."* For the Christian who is wholly surrendered to Jesus Christ as Lord, his or her life is transformed and that transformation is the direct result of his or her mind being "renewed." To think with a mind renewed by the Holy Spirit is to think clearly and thoroughly biblically. Such a mind is submitted to the authority of God's Word, having a great desire to live by faith and in humble obedience to God's revealed truth. It was Harry Blamires who coined the phrase, "think Christianly." Such is the mind being constantly fed on Holy Scripture and, as a result, is thinking in harmony with the mind of God. It is little wonder then that having such a mind results in the life being *"transformed;"* it has to be, because the whole person has been *"presented"* as a *"living and holy sacrifice…to God"* (Rom. 12:1-3). Such thinking, Peter tells us, is "for the purpose of prayer." It is impossible to imagine a mind like this being prayerless. The Christian possesses such a mind, "for the purpose of prayer."

Peter, in his two New Testament letters has quite a bit to say about the mind. Remembering that his letters were written against a background of severe persecution gives added emphasis to the whole idea of having a mind in harmony with the mind of God. No Christian will ever be able to remain faithful to His Lord and Saviour in the fires of persecution other than by having such a mind. No, please don't breath a sigh of relief at this point thinking this does not apply to you because you are not being persecuted. First of all, if you really want to live a holy life, making a difference in your world for God's glory, you will be persecuted. *"Indeed, all who desire to live godly in Christ Jesus will be persecuted"* (2 Tim. 3:12). Being holy is not being weird, being holy is being like Jesus, filled with His life because He lives on the inside of you. To use the biblical picture, it is like being light in a dark world or salt in a corrupt one (Matthew 5:13-14). This is something far beyond being good. This means having about you, without necessarily being aware of it, a likeness to Jesus, having the same effect on your world as He had on His. As light He exposed the darkness and, as salt, he exposed and stopped the progress of corruption. Darkness hates light because it cannot exist in the presence of light; *"the light shines in the darkness, and the darkness did not comprehend (overpower) it"* (John 1:5). Salt is a well known preservative and, as such, halts the progress of corruption. Every day in our media we learn of good people making a difference by doing good things. Sometimes even people who are philanthropic make a difference even though their money may have been amassed by corrupt means. Very rarely, however, are we told about the many people who are making a difference because the salt and light quality of their lives is turning people away from corruption and darkness towards a life changing relationship with God through yielding their lives to the Lord Jesus Christ as personal Saviour and Lord. Because Paul and his colleagues came among the people of Thessalonica they *"turned to God from idols to serve the living and true God, and to wait for His Son from heaven, whom He raised from the dead, that is Jesus who rescues us from the wrath to come"* (1 Thess. 1:9-10). Such lives of light and salt do so much more that relieve physical suffering and need. They do so much more that help the poor man just so that he can be buried in a good suit. They do that, but through the light and saltiness of Christ in their lives they also help people to find peace, meaning to life and hope for eternity. We rarely read in the media about the Jews and Palestinians who are worshipping Jesus together in the bond of His peace; or of the trained suicide bombers who have been delivered from hatred through being led to faith in

Christ in Jerusalem; or of the prisoners who, although serving their sentences in prison have found freedom in their hearts and minds through being introduced to the Lord Jesus. We rarely hear of ordinary people who have been enabled to cope with monumental trials by being helped to allow the light of the presence of Jesus Christ into their lives and, as a result, into their trials. The papers did not carry the story of the lady who had come to know Jesus and who later had to face death from cancer. Her testimony in her closing days was, "you have to be where I am to know how real God can be."

Such lives of light and saltiness are the antithesis of darkness and corruption. Is it any wonder then that the powers of darkness and corruption hate them. Even good people who are doing good things hate it when a truly holy life exposes the fact that they need something more. Godly people understand they are in a battle with evil powers in our broken world. They recognize that this is the source of the persecution and suffering that comes their way. It is true to say that far more believers in Jesus world-wide are being persecuted than not. Going back to Peter's reason for being of "sound judgement" ("clear minded") as being, "so that you can pray", we see the importance of the support of fellow Christians in developing and remaining faithful in our prayer life. If things go on as they are in this present day, persecution will become more the norm, even in our western culture. It is on the increase even now. All kinds of people who are going through trials of various kinds are usually very open to have someone pray with them. There is no doubt that real persecution will set most church prayer meetings alight with new fervency and purpose. How sad, and how grieving to the Holy Spirit, that we have to wait for persecution to stimulate our prayer lives.

Scripture says, ."..*let us consider how to stimulate one another to love and good deeds, not forsaking our own assembling together, as is the habit of some, but **encouraging one another**, and all the more as you see the day drawing near*" (Heb. 10:24-25). No real Christian can survive very long without becoming discouraged if they neglect being part of a local church. God has designed it that we function best as believers in the context of local churches

31

because, in so many ways, not least in the exercise of prayer, we need one another for mutual support and encouragement.

Again I emphasize that while on an individual level, biblical illiteracy is the number one malaise in the Christian church, constant church hopping and not being truly planted in a live Bible believing church is a close second. The reason for all the complaining about churches not meeting our needs and being lifeless is that many of our churches are prayerless. Very few of us really believe the word of Jesus when He said, *."...apart from Me you can do nothing"* (John 15:5) and this unbelief is nowhere more obvious than in so many church gatherings which are no more than apologies for prayer meetings. By and large such meetings lack passion, urgency even desperation. O that we really believed that all our organization, all our programs, all our academic achievements mean very little when it comes to the power of the Holy Spirit being released among us. In so many churches the Holy Spirit is grieved because sin is so often swept under the rug and left without being dealt with in brokenness and humility through biblical discipline. *"If I regard wickedness in my heart the Lord will not hear"* (Ps. 66:18). When Paul wrote to the church in Corinth it was a church full of potential yet because of things like divisiveness, immorality and legalism was highly dysfunctional. In encouraging the Corinthian Christians to deal with such evil Paul uses leaven as a picture of sin; just as *"a little leaven leavens the whole lump of dough"* (1 Cor. 5:6). When sin is left under the rug without ever being dealt with in a godly biblical fashion the whole life of the local church is adversely affected. In the strongest language Paul urges the church to *"clean out the old leaven so that you may be a new lump"* (1 Cor. 5:7). The expression, *"clean out"* is from the Greek word meaning to purge or to clean thoroughly. The results of such honesty, humility and faithfulness before the holiness of God is, "a new lump"; dough with no leaven; a church with no unconfessed sin; a church pure and renewed in oneness, joy and effectiveness because Christ reigns supreme as Lord and Head of His body.

Such a church is permeated with the presence of the living Christ. The love among the believers is very evident as is their joy in the Lord. Growth is no longer by transference from some other church but by people from the local community being brought to faith in Christ through the powerful witness of such a renewed community of Christians. My family belonged to such a church during my early teenage years. The experience is indelibly written on my memory. The purging process was deep and painful but thorough. The resulting revival was like a night to day transformation. The tears of repentance were replaced with tears of joy. The blessing God poured out on that little community of believers was extravagant. Believers were growing in their walk with God like never before. People from the surrounding community were coming to faith in Christ, being baptized and added to that local church. One of the most memorable features of that time was the prayer meetings. They were full. People were literally on their knees in God's presence. There was passion and tears of compassion as we pleaded with God for His protection and for the salvation of more and more lost souls in the village. People who were usually nothing more than seat warmers became involved by discovering and using their God given gifts. Such discoveries were made as they gravitated towards whatever aspect of the life of the church drew them. You see, no church will ever meet your needs until you are meeting its needs by using your God given gift or gifts.

O that we would all be of "sound judgement" ("clear minded"). Or as Peter puts it in another place, that we would, *"prepare [our] minds for action, keep sober in spirit, fix [our] hope completely on the grace to be brought to [us] at the revelation of Jesus Christ"* (1 Pet. 1:13). Or again, *"...I am stirring up your sincere mind by way of reminder..."* (2 Pet. 3:1).

Challenge

Let no excuse for prayerlessness stand in your way. Determine to soak yourself in God's word because out of that exercise your prayer life will develop. If you are praying about planting yourself in a local group of believers find out how high prayer is on their list of priorities. And I don't mean by giving it lip service but that it actually is a community of believers among whom prayer

33

is being made constantly; where every aspect of the life and ministry of the church is being bathed in prayer.

If you already belong to a church and you are conscious of a lamentable lack of earnest and believing prayer begin to take up the challenge by putting your own prayer life in order. Then humbly and graciously share your vision for prayer with the leadership, being willing to take the lead yourself in implementing a new vision for prayer.

THREE

Constantly Living in the Will of God

Another much needed quality "for the purpose of prayer" is, not only being "of sound judgement" ("clear minded"), but also being of "sober spirit." This word "sober" is from the Greek word meaning "to be free from the influence of intoxicants" it is used "in association" with watchfulness.[5] In other words I cannot be watchful and alert while under the influence of some intoxicant. Being honest with ourselves will reveal that, to a greater extent than we may be prepared to admit, we are intoxicated with things and stuff. It may be things like sports, shopping, movies etc; things which may not be wrong in and of themselves, but which have become out of balance in priorities. There may also be other things which are downright wrong and unhealthy to which we can become addicted. You see, we are called to be disciples of Jesus and not part time Christians. If my life is cluttered with the distractions offered by the world around me, the last thing I will want to do is pray, either alone or in the company of fellow Christians. In no sense is this kind of thinking negative, spoiling the fun. It is thinking that resonates with the person who is truly sick of the emptiness of what the world has to offer, and who is now totally free in Christ. Such a person has a new reason for living and, for the first time, real hope for the future. There is now purpose in the present and happy anticipation for the future.

If it may be said that being of "sound judgement" is the intellectual aspect of our preparation to pray effectively, being of "sober spirit" is the spiritual aspect. The NIV translates this

---

5   W. E. Vine; *Expository Dictionary of N.T. Words*; Oliphants Ltd, 1961 "sober"

expression as "self controlled." In other words the emphasis is now on having a true understanding of why we are here and where we are going. Why we are here; because Christ's work on the cross was to free us from sin so that our lives could now be lived for the will of God. Where we are going; because the people around us who do not yet know Christ are all going to meet the Lord as judge one day (1 Pet. 4:1-6).

Robert was fabulously wealthy. He was able to do whatever took his fancy at any time. He was making so much money that it didn't seem to matter how fast he spent it. The money just kept pouring in. He was able to drink without becoming an alcoholic and to dabble in drugs without becoming addicted. It was nothing to him to spend many thousands of dollars to rent a helicopter and pilot for a day just to take his son to Alaska to see the Grisly bears. His life style was lavish. Why was it he found himself in his luxurious home in the San Francisco Bay area one evening holding a gun to his temple ready to take his own life? His lifestyle may have been lavish but his life was empty. Just as he was about to pull the trigger the voice of a television preacher caught his attention. He put the gun down, listened to the preacher tell him how Christ died as his substitute taking the judgement of God that ought to have been his. Robert turned his life over to the Lord Jesus as his Saviour and Lord right there in his living room. "Immediately, every cell in my body became aware of the presence of God" was his testimony. Robert went out and bought a Bible and began reading it voraciously; all the time "drinking tequila and snorting coke." But he was a changed man. Soon the booze and the drugs were flushed down the toilet. He very quickly became active in his local church. When I met him his greatest joy was to tell the world about the transformation in his life through meeting Christ for himself. He also loved to communicate his excitement over the coming again of the Lord Jesus. Robert really came alive when he met Christ. He was a truly joyful man and a beautiful example of what it means to be of *"sound judgement and sober spirit."* The past was forgiven, the present was full of meaning, and the future was full of what the Bible calls, *"sure and steadfast"* hope (Heb. 6:19).

When Paul was instructing some Christians about this kind of quality living (1 Thess. 4:3-8) he points out that such a life is only possible because of the resources God has provided through the Holy Spirit who was given to live in each believer in Jesus. This quality of life is not an outer improvement. It is an inner transformation brought about by the Holy Spirit living His life in and through the surrendered life of each Christian. This means Jesus does not just tell us to be holy, He is that holiness living inside us. Oswald Chambers put it so well when he said, "if all Jesus Christ can do is to tell me I must be holy, His teaching plants despair."[6] It is now a question of surrendering to Jesus and thus allowing Him to be holy in me and through me.

Galatians 5:23 teaches us that *"self control"* is part of the fruit of the Spirit. In other words it is something the Holy Spirit reproduces in the Christian and through the Christian every day. This throws new light on Jesus teaching in Matthew 5:20 where He says, *"For I say to you that unless your righteousness surpasses that of the scribes and Pharisees, you will not enter the kingdom of heaven."* The Pharisees were the strictest sect among the Jews. The point in Jesus words is that to exceed their teaching is impossible apart from the supernatural resource of the Holy Spirit living in the Christian. This is clearly laid out again in Romans 8:3-4. Christ, *"as an offering for sin, He condemned sin in the flesh, so that the requirements of the law might be fulfilled in us, who do not walk according to the flesh but according to the Spirit."* The late Major Ian Thomas, founder of the Torchbearer movement, used to say, "the Christian life is not hard, its impossible." What he meant of course was that the only way true godliness can be realized is through the power of the indwelling Holy Spirit. This is what Jesus was getting at in John 15:8 when He said, *"My Father is glorified by this, that you bear much fruit, **and so prove to be My disciples.**"* The context is teaching that a branch on a vine cannot produce grapes by itself; it produces the fruit because it is part of the vine and the life of the vine is flowing through it. So, as disciples of Jesus, we cannot produce

---

6   Oswald Chambers; *My Utmost for His Highest*

Christ-likeness by ourselves but only by being totally surrendered to Him allowing His life to flow through us.

All this ought to leave us in no doubt as to why it is impossible to live as a man or woman of God in isolation. We need one another. In the light of biblical teaching it is difficult to imagine how any Christian who is full of all God has done for them in Christ, would even want to live in isolation.

We all have had disappointments. People have let us down from time to time. But the issues at stake are far too important to simply overlook or try to forget. There is little point in trying to be a healthy member of a body while detached from the body. It simply will not work. There are times we all need to humble ourselves acknowledging that our position of isolation is not the will of God. We must leave all the hurt at the foot of the cross and be restored to a healthy relationship with God's people in a local church. It is possible to rediscover how powerful in God's hands a praying church can be.

As we will see in the next section of this book the only way a healthy church can function is for each member of the local body to be in harmonious relationship with all the others. If there is disunity, it becomes impossible to pray effectively either in private or in company with fellow believers. Sometimes sin, which causes disunity, has to be dealt with through church discipline but always with restoration in view (Gal. 6:1).

It is my earnest prayer that every reader of this book will be deeply impressed with the fact that both a prayerless Christian and a prayerless church are dysfunctional. Both are trying to function outside the will of God and, as a result will remain ineffective. Being truly alive to what is going on around us as the "end of all things" draws nearer is the greatest need of the hour in the Christian church. Perhaps sooner than any of us realize the Lord will return.

Challenge

Were Jesus to return today would you be happy to meet Him with your life in its present condition?

FOUR

Where Prayer is Alive and Effective

In all my years as a preacher of the gospel in the context of churches of varying denominations, I have never known a praying church that was not a growing church. A prayerless church is simply telling God He is not needed. Whereas a praying church is giving expression to the fact that its members truly believe, and don't just profess to believe the words of Jesus, *"apart from Me you can do nothing"* (John 15:5). It is my experience that being in God's word daily, absorbing its truth, produces a prayerful heart. There is no better way to bring depth and effectiveness to the prayer life than being soaked in the living and eternal truth of God's word and then turning that truth into prayer. In other words, praying God's word back to Him. It really is true that apart from Him we can do **NOTHING**. To see the power of God released among us only ever happens as a result of sacrificial prayer from hearts who know, beyond all doubt, that they are utterly dependent on God for anything of eternal value to happen. This is the only way a church will really grow with growth that is truly glorifying to the Lord. We need to learn to stop relying in personalities and demonstrate that we are depending on God.

The amusing story is told about the rooster who came into the chicken coop rolling an ostrich's egg ahead of him. The chickens were all sitting on their perches with eyes out like organ stops never having seen such a thing in their lives. "I just want you guys to know what is happening in other places," said the rooster. Today we will try all kinds of things to produce church growth including importing evidence of growth from other places thinking if only we could imitate the other places we would see the same results. Nothing could be further from the truth. Nothing can ever replace being on our faces before almighty God with a desperate realization of our helplessness apart from Him. You see, God wants us to "bloom where we are planted," as someone once said. The trouble is the devil has convinced so many of us that it can't be done; our community is too difficult. We can't imagine some of our neighbors and family members coming to faith in Christ. Our vision does not stretch to seeing the whole atmosphere in our local schools being transformed as school principals, teachers and students come to personally know Christ as Saviour and Lord. It never enters our heads that the local porn shops and casinos could be closed down and drug dealing cease because so many people in our community are coming to know Christ and, as a result, are being delivered from all kinds of addictions. We never imagine that people who are over their heads in debt could have their finances brought into line with God's plan and so be set free from that crippling burden and the emptiness of materialism as they surrender their lives to Christ as Lord. What is the answer? Is it that we parachute an evangelist in from outside? Is it, as one preacher said, to "subcontract our evangelism to Nicky Gumbel", even though tremendous things have resulted from the Alpha Course. No, no, no, a thousand times no; there is absolutely no substitute for the transformation of a personal prayer life and, as a result, that of a local church. When that happens we will be crying out to God in desperation, having acquired His heart for lost people, really believing that *"apart from [Him we] can do NOTHING."* The need of the hour is for God's almighty power to be released among us. There is no God consciousness in our communities because there is no God consciousness in our churches. We simply have to get this right because one thing is for sure; the way we are doing things at the moment simply is not working.

Above and beyond everything else, something will happen as a result of revolutionized prayer lives. At the personal level and, as a result, at the local church level, the Lord Jesus Christ will be front and centre in our minds, our devotion and our motivation. It is always the will of God that, as far as the Lord Jesus is concerned, *"He Himself will come to have first place in everything"* (Col. 1:18). That means to worship is to "forget about yourself and concentrate on Him", to quote the Bruce Ballinger song. It means minds focussed upon, *"the simplicity and purity of devotion to Christ"* (2 Cor. 11:3). All our motivation in service will be, *"we do not preach ourselves but Christ Jesus as Lord"* (2 Cor. 4:5). The world around us needs to know about Jesus and that will never happen until His people are really excited about knowing Him and are passionate about making Him known. Belonging to a powerfully praying church will light a fire in your soul, filling you with a deep desire to tell your story to all who will listen. The story which is yours alone, how you came to know Christ and what He means to you. In the community where there is a powerfully praying church there will be many God given opportunities to do just that. God will see to it. You will come from the presence of God with His glory upon you. The cashier at the check out, the waiter in the restaurant, will be aware of something different, even if you are unaware this is happening. People you meet every day will, sooner or later, be open to listen to your story. When you, *"sanctify Christ as Lord in your heart"*, you will, *"always be ready"* and people will want you to, *"give an account for the hope that is in you."* You will be so filled with Jesus that you will do this, *"with gentleness and reverence"* (1 Pet. 3:15).

Peter was following (Jesus) at a distance and later denying Him three times because earlier he was sleeping when he ought to have been praying; (see Luke 22). The greatest moment in Peter's life was when the rooster crowed following his third denial that he knew Jesus. At that moment Peter was completely broken as he was suddenly confronted with his terrible failure and the shame of it all. Without doubt this was the greatest moment in Peter's life. He was totally at an end of himself, in no doubt as to his utter weakness and powerlessness. Later this man who denied the Lord Jesus three times and, one of those times with oaths and curses, met the Lord Jesus now risen from the dead. Three times; once for each denial, Jesus asked Peter, *"do you love Me?"* His answers seem to come from a greatly humbled and broken spirit, *"Lord, You know all things; You know that I love you."* It is so beautiful to watch Peter in the book of Acts after the Holy Spirit had been poured out at Pentecost. Everything he did was bathed in prayer. He was a man of prayer who demonstrated that he was now totally convinced he could not even begin to be the man the Lord wanted him to be in his own strength. This new attitude was strengthened by his realization of his need of the prayer support of his brothers and sisters in Christ. Once, when he had seen the apostle James arrested and put to death, he himself was arrested and thrown into prison. Peter must have thought he was next for execution. Acts 12 tells the story of his miraculous deliverance from prison and makes it very clear that all the time God was at work, *"prayer for [Peter] was being made fervently by the church to God"* (Acts 12:5). It might have been a very different story had Peter been going it alone. By the way, if you are anything like me, when you run into health challenges, family crises or situations beyond you're control, you are glad to think brothers and sisters in Christ are praying for you.

What will it take for this message to penetrate the minds and hearts of God's people in our western culture. From my experience, the persecuted church has so much to teach us. I will never forget teaching for a week in a small Bible School in Kampala, Uganda. All the young students had suffered terribly because they loved Jesus. One young man who had witnessed his parents being murdered because of their devotion to Christ constantly lived with the knowledge that those same persecutors were looking for him too. One of the girls had been cruelly abused by the "soldiers" in the "Lord's Resistance Army." She had been able, by God's grace, to forgive those who abused her and was radiant with new life in Jesus. The lasting memory of those students is one of the "simplicity and purity of their devotion to Christ." I was moved to tears each time I had the privilege of worshipping with them. They knew what it meant to really pray. I will never forget hearing them out in the court yard which surrounded the premises used for the school. It was 5 am and there they were crying to the Lord, pleading with Him with tears as they prayed for one another and for the situation in Uganda and Sudan. People are more responsive to the gospel in that part of the world. But why is that? Having witnessed the situation with my own eyes I believe it has all to do with the fact that our African brothers and sisters know what it means to be desperate in prayer; to lay hold of God with prayer and fasting, being fully convinced that apart from Him they can do nothing. Because those precious people prayed as they did, when we went with them to many of the huge refugee settlements in Uganda and Sudan and preached the gospel, people came to Christ in large numbers. Some of those were delivered from evil spirits. God moves when His people pray, of that there is no doubt. Prayer always draws us into deeper communion with the Lord. The first person to be changed through praying is the person praying. God becomes more real; the appreciation of His majesty and power grows; faith is increased and God's heart for lost people is imparted in prayer. There is absolutely no doubt about the fact that the kind of church that makes a difference in any community is a praying church.

Being prayerless is the area of greatest weakness in most of our western churches. If you are looking for a church where you can simply settle down and be comfortable; where the normal routine of your life will be undisturbed; where you will rarely be challenged; where you want very little other than your kids are being entertained and kept out of the drug scene; where your beautiful daughter or one in a million son will find a suitable life partner (remember its not enough that the chosen spouse is a professing Christian) **then this is exactly the kind of church you need.** In this kind of church you will be challenged out of your comfort zone; you will be challenged to examine and, sometimes, radically adjust priorities in your "normal" routine. In fact there may be a new normal. Your kids will be less likely to rebel and make wrong choices in this kind of church. Notice I said, less likely. Sometimes even in the godliest of families there are rebellious teenagers. The point is, in this kind of church, you will discover what it means to joyfully abide in Christ, no matter what, and you will, as a result, be able to say like the Psalmist David said, *"My soul finds rest in God alone...."* (Ps. 62:1 NIV). If you have not realized it yet, you will one day; "reality spoils life." Any Christian who thinks he or she can go it alone without being planted in a local church is delusional. We are all part of a very broken world which is heading for divine judgement. The Bible makes it very clear that, as Christians, members of Christ's body, the church, we are called to be in the world but not of it. Our lives can no longer be dominated by the values and value system of this present age. See 1 John 2:15-17). Listen to the Lord Jesus as He prayed for His disciples, then and now, and for the world,

> *"I have given them Your word; and the world has hated them, because they are not of the world, even as I am not of the world. I do not ask you to take them out of the world, but to keep them from the evil one. They are not of the world, even as I am not of the world, Sanctify them in Your truth; Your word is truth. As you sent Me into the world, I also have sent them into the world"* (John 17:14-18).

In the context of this wonderful High Priestly prayer of the Lord Jesus in John chapter 17 He prayed for His disciples that, *"they may be one."* He made it clear that this oneness was the same oneness as that between Himself and His Father. One of the great provisions God has made for us as members of Christ's body, the church, is vibrant and stimulating fellowship with others who love the Lord. When Hebrews 10:25 instructs us about, *"not forsaking our own assembling together,"* the context is that of, *"how to stimulate on another to love and good deeds."* No believer in Jesus can grow as God wants them to grow apart from active and regular fellowship in a local church. Isolation brings loneliness and loneliness is fertile ground for temptation. The more a person tries to justify voluntary isolation from a local church, the more expert they become at justifying a lifestyle of compromise. Being part of a praying church is a tremendous safeguard against such compromise and the resulting spiritual weakness.

Some years ago I had the privilege of meeting the late Geoffrey Bull, author of *When Iron Gates Yield* and *The Sky is Red*. Mr. Bull had gone as a missionary to Tibet. While there that country was invaded by the Chinese Communist Army. Mr. Bull was arrested and for a large part of his three years in prison was in solitary confinement or, if you like, enforced isolation. He endured the mental torture of "re-education and thought reform." All the time he was in prison God's people throughout the world were praying for him. I recall how, shortly after his release, he was to speak to a crowd of those who had prayed for him. Seeing all the people so soon after prolonged isolation was too overwhelming and he had to leave the platform. I met him some years after this and one of the rich memories I have of this humble man of God is the appreciation he had for his brothers and sisters in Christ. One of the things which sustained and strengthened him through that long ordeal was the prayers of fellow Christians. Another was the word of God, especially the parts he had committed to memory. Whether we like it or not, we need one another if we plan on growing and becoming the men and women God wants us to be. At some time or other in life we will all have to face personal crisis. It is such a source of encouragement in such times knowing you belong to a local church, where caring fellow Christians are holding you up in prayer. One of the things my wife and I have been most grateful for over the many years in the ministry of preaching the gospel is the prayer support of so many in the wider body of Christ, as well as those in the local churches to which we have belonged.

Jesus teaching in Luke 18 was *"to show that at all times they ought to pray and not to lose heart"* (v. 1). Later in the New Testament Paul challenges his readers to *"pray without ceasing"* (1 Thess. 5:17). In other words their whole experience of living as members of His body ought to be in the atmosphere of constant prayer. Growth in our relationship with the Lord is impossible without prayer; personal and in fellowship with others. James Montgomery's beautiful hymn expresses this idea perfectly:

Prayer is the Christian's vital breath,
the Christian's native air,
Our watchword at the gates of death;
We enter heaven with prayer.

The saints in prayer appear as one
In word and deed and mind,
While with the Father and the Son
Sweet fellowship they find.

For someone from the western church scene, it came as a tremendous challenge when, in a house church prayer meeting in China, my friend saw a sheet hanging on a wall in the prayer room which said, "Don't say anything in here you are not prepared to die for." Those Chinese believers prayed together constantly aware of the possibility of infiltrators being present. Paul taught the Ephesian Christians that *"our struggle is not against flesh and blood, but against the rulers, against the powers, against the world forces of this darkness, against the spiritual forces of wickedness in the heavenly places"* (Eph. 6:12). In the context of urging them to put on *"the whole armor of God"* Paul makes it clear that everything has to be constantly covered with prayer. *"With all prayer and petition pray at all times in the Spirit, and with this in view, be on the alert with all perseverance and petition for all the saints"* (Eph. 6:18).

I have often thought I could never stand up to the kind of persecution being endured by so many of my brothers and sisters in Christ throughout the world, both in New Testament times and today. Then I read scriptures like Isaiah 40:31, *"Yet those who wait for the Lord will gain new strength; they will mount up with wings like eagles, they will run and not get tired, they will walk and not become weary."* The words "gain new" or, as other translations have it, "renew", are interesting. They can be translated, "change" as in changing garments, or "in exchange for."[7] This is immensely encouraging and I submit to you, this kind of effective praying is partly a personal exercise but also a corporate one. Remember Paul's words in Ephesians 6:18, quoted above, *"for all the saints."* To imagine I can survive spiritually on my own and that I don't really need to pray in

---

7   Harris, Laird, Waltke, *Theological Wordbook of the Old Testament*, Moody Press, Chicago, 1980

the context of fellowship with local believers exhibits a very subtle but real selfish arrogance. Isolation from the body of believers always results in spiritual weakness.

It is true, we are not yet suffering physical persecution to any marked degree in our western culture. All the more reason, therefore, to be planted in a praying church locally so that we can encourage one another in facing whatever challenges come our way as God's people. "Only turning God's house into a house of fervent prayer will reverse the power of evil so evident in the world today" (Jim Cymbala).

The story of the Old Testament Prophet Elijah in 1 Kings 17 and 18 has always been a favorite of mine. The king on the throne of Israel at the time was Ahab. He was not the kind of man you would want in your circle of close friends. The moral decline in the nation during his reign was at an all time low; *"Ahab the son of Omri did evil in the sight of the LORD more than all who were before him"* (16:30). *"Thus Ahab did more to provoke the Lord God of Israel than all the kings of Israel who were before him"* (16:33). There is little doubt that, in our western world, we are at an all time low morally. The need of the hour is for God's people, as Elijah did in his day, to stand against this tide in the name of Almighty God. Notice the stages of this battle against the tide of evil:

Elijah boldly identified himself with Almighty God, *"As the LORD the God of Israel lives before whom I stand ..."* (17:1). Elijah knew his God and was not afraid to say so. Are we there? Not until Christ is Lord in our lives will we ever be. (See 1 Pet. 3:15).

Elijah was prepared to trust God for every detail in the process, *"Go...and hide yourself by the brook Cherith...It shall be that you will drink of the brook, and I have commanded the ravens to provide for you there"* (17:3-4). On a scale of 1-10 where would you put our experiential level of confidence in God? We all love to quote Ephesians 3:20, *"Now to Him Who is able to do far more abundantly beyond all that we ask or think, **according to the power that works within us**..."* That last phrase is a bit embarrassing is it not?

Elijah went and God did as promised! He drank from the brook and the ravens brought his food (17:4-6). When the brook dried up God sent him to a widow in Zarephath where God had commanded the widow to provide Elijah's food. Again he went, and because of his obedience that widow's life was never the same again. The meagre resources she had when given over to God were multiplied for as long as the famine lasted and a family tragedy became a huge faith strengthener (17:14-24).

Elijah was now even more prepared to face Ahab and the evil in the nation. God's next command took his obedience to a new level, *"Go show yourself to Ahab"* (18:1). I don't know if the widow from Zarephath heard about this or not but I can just imagine her excitement, I can see her jumping up and down and yelling, "way to go LORD, way to go Elijah!" Whether Elijah, the widow or you and me, the only thing that strengthens faith is obedience. *"And without faith it is **impossible** to please Him, for he who comes to God must believe that He is and that **He is a rewarder of those who seek Him**"* (Heb. 11:6).

When he met Ahab, the king blamed the man of God for all the trouble the nation was in (18:17). First century AD Christians were looked upon as social misfits and some of them were blamed for the great fire of Rome. 21st century Christians are considered right wing bigots who are a constant hindrance to post modern progress. What will the next phase be for us or the next generation?

Elijah, who knew God and had proved Him stood firm and confronted the real issue, *"you have forsaken the commandments of the LORD and you have followed the Baals"* (18:18). As it was then, so it is today; the real issue is, *"if the LORD is God, follow Him: but if Baal, follow him"* (18:21). Is anyone or anything other than the LORD taking first place in your life or mine today?

How was such a dilemma to be sorted out? By each party calling upon their God and which ever one answers will be the real one and the only one worth following. The stage was set. The prophets of Baal went first. They prepared their offering for their god and began their particular ritual. They continued all morning *"but there was no voice and no one answered"* (18:26). By this time they were becoming desperate and, to make matters worse, Elijah, in his total confidence in the living God, began mocking them and suggesting Baal might be deaf or asleep or off on holiday! The silly thing is, the prophets of Baal actually took Elijah seriously. They were beginning to believe Baal was deaf because they began calling on him *"with a loud voice"* (18:28). They then worked themselves into a total frenzy (who are the fanatics now?), cutting themselves and continuing to rave on until evening. When it was obvious Baal was a loser Elijah calmly took over in the name of the LORD. He went to the root of all Israel's problems and *"repaired the alter of the LORD which had been torn down"* (18:30). The nation was in such trouble because they had dethroned God. Again, as it was then, so it is today, godlessness leads to ruin. (See Ephesians 5:3-6), *"Let no one deceive you with empty words, for because of these things the wrath of God comes upon the sons of disobedience."* Elijah next prepared his offering for the LORD, dug a trench around the alter and, three times, requested that water be poured over the thing he was expecting God to set alight. When his offering was well and truly soaked he calmly and confidently made his request of the LORD revealing, in the process, what his real motives were, *"that this people may know that You, O LORD, are God, and that you have turned their heart back again"* (18:37).

It worked! *"The fire of the LORD fell and consumed the burnt offering and the wood and the stones and the dust and licked up the water that was in the trench"* (18:38). The evidence was totally compelling. When God works no one is in any doubt who is behind what is happening. No one that day had the slightest grounds for taking any credit. All the glory was the LORD'S. *"They fell on their faces; and they said, 'the LORD He is God; the LORD He is God'"* (18:39).

When the evil prophets of Baal had been done away with Elijah was ready for the next step; showing what God will do when all sin has been repented of, renounced and everything to do with it put away. The whole nation, even the environment was positively affected. Oh, if we could only see what could happen were the churches to really learn the power of prayer.

All that remained now was to watch what God would do. The rains came. The famine was over.

What does all this have to do with us? *"Elijah **was a man with a nature like ours, AND HE PRAYED EARNESTLY** that it would not rain, and it did not rain on the earth for three years and six months. Then **he prayed again,** and the sky poured rain and the earth produced its fruit"* (Jam. 5:17-18). Not only was Elijah a man with a nature like ours but **his God is our God. Nothing about God or His power has changed.**

Can such things still happen? "A few months ago while on a ministry trip to the UK I had the privilege of meeting up with some friends I had not seen for some years. Together we went for a long walk which turned out to be a rich fellowship time. The main topic of conversation was, believe it or not, how the churches in their locality were joining together to pray out of a real concern for the spiritual well-being of the community. Things were going badly wrong and the authorities were at their wits end. As a result of the prayer action being taken by the churches things began to change. Things changed to such an extent that the prayer involvement of the churches now figures prominently in the new thinking among those in authority."

I have considerable sympathy for you when you say, but there is no church in my locality where this kind of praying is the norm. Most church prayer meetings are so lacking in passion and therefore so boring it is little wonder so few people attend. Can anything be done?

Challenge

If you already attend a church prayer group, seek God as to why our churches are so weak in the area of prayer. This will help create a spirit of deep repentance and renewal

Instead of the older generation being so critical of young people, cry to God that they will be protected from messing up their generation like we have messed up ours. This again will result in a spirit of deep repentance and humbling ourselves in God's presence.

Consider having someone whose ministry is prayer and intercession to lead a weekend of teaching on the subject.

Form "Prayer Triplets" in the church - three people or three couples each praying for three other people or three other couples. Each triplet will meet regularly. Each triplet will respect confidentiality. This simple exercise will add urgency and expectancy to your church's prayer ministry.

SECTION 2

I Need A Church

Because I need to learn how to love fervently and to be loved
1 Peter 4:8-9

Something To Think About...

You may have heard the old adage, "Prayer changes things." While this is true, the first thing to change as a result of real prayer is the one doing the praying. For example, if you have something against another brother or sister in Christ and you pray it through in God's presence, you will be challenged in the areas where your own heart needs to change. Oswald Chambers once said, "prayer is getting hold of God and not the answer." Getting hold of God cannot happen without total honesty in His presence. This results in total surrender to Him as Lord which leads to being filled with His Spirit and His love being, *"poured out within our hearts through the Holy Spirit who is given to us"* (Rom. 5:5).

FIVE

Such Love is Vital

Do you attend this church regularly?

"I have been drawn to attend this church because the people who worship here really love one another."

This brief conversation was one I had with a lady I met at the door of a church where I was to preach that particular Sunday morning. What an encouragement as I prepared to bring God's word to that congregation.

You need to be part of a local church because this is the only way Christians can demonstrate that they truly are disciples of Christ. Why else would Peter use the words he did in verse 8, *"Above all keep fervent in your love for one another"*? When Jesus taught His disciples about loving one another His words were so far reaching.

"A new commandment I give to you, that you love one another, even as I have loved you, that you also love one another. By this all men will know that you are my disciples, if you have love for one another" (John 13:34-35).

Peter's words "above all" carry the meaning, 'prior to' or 'before anything else'. In other words the quality of life in any local church and the measure of its effectiveness must never be thought of only in terms of how lively the worship is or in terms of the numbers attending. The bottom line is the extent to which the supernatural love of Christ is being reproduced in the lives of those claiming to be His disciples. Remember, Jesus standard is, *"as I have loved you...."* This is what makes the disciples of Christ so distinct in any community. Apart from this a local church is no different from any other group of people meeting at the golf club or the local pub for that matter.

It is no exaggeration to say that the kind of expression of Christ's love seen in John 13:34-35 quoted above, is impossible in isolation. Trying to survive spiritually in isolation is therefore completely unbiblical.

But where am I ever to find such a church you may be asking? You can be forgiven for not believing such a church exists anywhere. You may be tempted to give up the search right here feeling the biblical standard is impossible to attain. That is just the point. It is impossible. It was the late Major Ian Thomas who once said (quoted above), "the Christian life is not hard, it's impossible." What he meant was the standard set by the Lord Jesus cannot be attained apart from Christ Himself living His life in the disciple and consequently Christ loving through the disciple. This only begins to happen when you and I are truly His disciples; truly surrendered to Him as Lord. Now, Peter had not lost touch with reality when he wrote verse 8. No, he was well aware of the humanness of the people to whom he was writing. That is why he added the phrase, ."....*because love covers a multitude of sins.*" We are all frail human beings and far from perfect. But the point is, the surrendered life, growing in Christ, becomes an increasingly selfless life. The disciple becomes much more concerned about the well being of his or her brothers or sisters in Christ's body than about homing in on the faults we all see in one another. Take it from me, when you have been around churches of various stripes for as long as I have you will know there are times when it sure is hard to love the saints. Yet, at the same time, they are the most unique and wonderful people you will ever meet. When I was lying in hospital three years ago having just had open heart surgery Psalm 16 came alive in a new way for me. Verse 3 says, "*as for the saints who are in the earth, they are the majestic ones in whom is all my delight.*" I was deeply moved just thinking about how my life has been so enriched just by being among God's people. The beautiful account of the life of Ruth, one of the great women of the Bible, has something to say to us here. There is a particularly moving moment when Ruth makes her life changing decision to stay with her mother in law Naomi who was pressing her to return to her own people. "*But Ruth said, Do not urge* *me to leave you or turn back from following you, for where you go, I will go, and where you lodge, I will lodge. **Your people shall be my people,** and your God, my God. Where you die, I will die, and there I will be buried. Thus may the Lord do to me, and worse, if anything but death parts you and me"* (Ruth 1:16, 17). Ruth went on to marry Boaz and we know from the genealogy of the Lord Jesus in Matthew chapter 1 that Jesus, as far as His legal, earthly parents were concerned, descended through that line; see Matthew 1:5. Ruth's commitment to stay with Naomi is a beautiful picture of what the Christian's commitment to Christ ought to be like. Part of that commitment is that **His people shall be my people.** Being, by the grace of God, in that relationship with His people has the potential to be the most enriching of life's experiences. That is exactly what is in Peter's mind in challenging us as to our relationship with one another.

The disciples concern is *"building up and not destroying"* (see 2 Cor. 10:8). Sins that are covered by this quality of love are not covered because they have been swept under the rug. Under the rug may mean out of sight but they are certainly not out of mind; neither the sinner's nor the Lord's. The supernatural love of Christ in the surrendered heart will result in sins and failings being dealt with humbly and honestly and with a true desire to build one another up. Sometimes there has to be the painful experience for the church leadership to exercise godly discipline. Galatians 6:1 makes it clear that such discipline can only be administered by those who are "spiritual" and only in a spirit of "gentleness" remembering how easily one can also be tempted. The aim of all such discipline ought always to be to "restore." When Paul wrote to Timothy about, *"keeping faith and a good conscience,"* he spoke of people, like Hymenaeus and Alexander who, seeming to be unteachable, had *"rejected such things"* and, as a result had *"suffered shipwreck in regard to their faith."* There was no sweeping of such things under any rugs. As far as those two difficult people were concerned Paul spoke of them as those *"whom I have handed over to Satan, so that they will be taught not to blaspheme"* (1 Tim. 1:19-20; see also 1 Cor. 5:5). Dr. Donald Guthrie suggests that, "handed over to Satan" means "no more than that they are put out of the church into

Satan's province (i.e. the non-Christian world)." Then he adds, "the concluding clause, 'that they may learn not to blaspheme' shows clearly that the purpose was remedial and not punitive. However stringent the process the motive was mercy, and whenever ecclesiastical discipline has departed from this purpose of restoration, its hardness has proved a barrier to progress. But this is no reason for dispensing with discipline entirely, a failing which frequently characterizes our modern churches." [8]

My experience of seeing church discipline administered in the spirit of Galatians 6:1 is that it was done with tears on the part of the leadership administering it and it had an awesome effect on the rest of the congregation. We learned something about just how sinful sin really is and how much the Holy Spirit is grieved by it. We also learned something about the Holiness of God and what it means to "fear" Him.

Does this seem to you to be rather harsh? Isn't there an easier way? Can't we just lighten up a bit? When we realize the issues at stake, like the world around us understanding we, as Christians, are Christ's disciples and the local church being the living expression of the life of Christ, then the bar can never be set too high. This is why, I believe, Peter begins with prayer. He knows full well that seeking the Lord in prayer will have a deep effect on the life of the church. Every other aspect of its life will be affected. Whatever church you become part of, or are already part of, will never be perfect but I urge you to take Peter's words seriously and, rather than focussing on the shortcomings of others, seek God in earnest prayer till the reproduction of the love of Christ in your church becomes the number one focus of all that goes on there. This will not mean you will just be a happy little group enjoying one long holy huddle. It will mean that Christ's love among you will be so dynamic that the whole community will know you are His disciples. Through the witness of such a church people will be led to faith in Christ and to being baptized. They will then become expressions of His love as they in their turn serve in the local church.

---

8   Donald Guthrie, B.D., M.Th. *The Pastoral Epistles: An Introduction and Commentary*, The Tyndale Press, May 1961, Pages 68 and 69

Something is missing today because this is simply not happening to the degree it ought to be happening. For a church to become this dynamic and this effective in witness there is a need for an infusion of the love of Christ. Again I emphasize, we are talking about the actual love of Christ being reproduced in His people. Just imagine for a moment what that would look like. We would be more aware of God than of one another. People coming among us from the community would come to understand what God consciousness meant. Not only would they sense God's love in the place but they would be made deeply aware that something was missing from their own lives and families. That is called coming under the convicting power of the Holy Spirit. The tragedy is that in today's western church we have very little idea of what it means to have the glory of God among us. People ought never to be able to visit our churches and leave unaffected. So many churches today have all the doctrinal pieces in place but, tragedy of tragedies, something vital in missing.

When Paul wrote to the Colossian church he was dealing with stuff like doctrinal compromise and deceptive philosophy, see chapter 2 verse 8. In dealing with such things his great passion was to point them again to the Lord Jesus in whom all that God is lives, *"in bodily form"* (Col. 2:9), and in whom they, *"have been made complete"* (Col. 2:10). Indeed he points them to Jesus, *"who is our life"* (Col. 3:4). It is the reality of that life which the Lord wants to reveal to the world through us His people. While it is very important to be doctrinally biblical, that by itself simply will not cut it. Without the infusion of God's all pervading, transforming love, churches will continue to be the kind of places many people don't want anything to do with.

Even as I write a vivid reminder of something I saw on my visit to South Sudan comes to mind. The people wanted to build a hospital and they worked so hard to make bricks. All over the site where the hospital was to be built were huge piles of bricks. Every brick was made by hand; no effort had been spared. The hospital was there in potential but grass and weeds grew profusely all around the piles of bricks. Why had the work ceased? There was nothing to hold the bricks together. They had no cement. The people had played their part but unless this great need was met from somewhere else, the piles of bricks would never reach their potential. The New Testament teaching about the church is that it is made up of *"living stones"* (1 Pet. 2:5) and not man made bricks. Each stone is created by God; built into that *"spiritual house"* which is the church. Here my illustration about the bricks breaks down. But, please bear with me.

Allow me to quote extensively here from Paul's writing to the Colossian church, *"So as those who have been chosen of God, holy and beloved, put on a heart of compassion, kindness, humility, gentleness and patience; bearing with one another, and forgiving each other, whoever has a complaint against anyone; just as the Lord forgave you, so also should you.* **Beyond all these things put on love, which is the perfect bond of unity"** (Col. 3:12-14).

The word "beyond" (v. 14) carries with the meaning, 'above' or 'over'. All the challenges listed in verses 12 and 13 are all things with which we are so familiar. They highlight the things which bring disunity. We are so familiar with them because *"the perfect bond of unity"* is so often missing. And what is that perfect bond? It is that quality of love which is the only thing able to deal with all the divisive things which destroy the distinctiveness which ought to be in evidence among people who claim to be disciples of Jesus.

Back to the piles of bricks! The hospital could not be built so as to bring physical healing to the community of Kajo Keji, South Sudan because that which could have joined those bricks together in unity was missing.

It has been well said that the church exists for the benefit of those outside its walls. It is high time we faced facts. Such people are not drawn to many churches because, the *"love which is the perfect bond of unity"* simply is not in evidence as it ought to be. The Corinthian church, with all its gifting had to be faced with the challenge, *"if I have the gift of prophecy, and know all mysteries and all knowledge; and if I have all faith, so as to remove mountains, but do not have love, I am nothing"* (1 Cor. 13:2). As you think about this, does it not break your heart? Perhaps you are one of those who have been deeply hurt by some of the goings on in churches. Perhaps you can look back to better days spiritually, but that *"first love"* (Rev. 2:4) has cooled somewhat. Perhaps you find it very difficult to commit to a local church because of the disappointments you are dealing with. Please allow me to encourage you to think again; to take it all to the cross where Jesus died for sin in all its shapes and forms. There is healing and renewal there. You see, the great need of the hour in our 21st century is for a mighty revival, a visitation of God in all His power and glory; a revival of such magnitude that such a new God awareness would come to the church again and that it would flow out to the communities around. O that all of God's people would be on their knees before Him in humility and repentance, pleading for God to come among us again in revival power.

Challenge

Be encouraged to humble yourself with a willingness to seek the Lord and be renewed in your walk with Him, which will be accompanied by a desire to renew fellowship with God's people in some local church where you live. My own father was renewed in his walk with God after living as an isolated Christian for 37 years. One of the first things that happened following his relationship with the Lord being renewed, was that he returned to sharing in the life of his local church where he was warmly welcomed. Both he and the church were blessed.

SIX

Such Love is Radical

Has it dawned on you yet just how free you are in Christ as one of His disciples? It is impossible to live on this planet without being affected in one way or another by the things which affect everyone else just by being part of this very broken world. We are not immune from sickness, bereavement, loneliness, disappointment, temptation, pain, being a victim of crime, rejection, the list is almost endless. But one thing is certain, no matter what comes our way, as disciples of Christ we have the freedom to choose what to do with whatever we are facing. For example, someone may have hurt you very badly either by something they said or by their attitude towards you. As a disciple of Jesus, one in whose life He is Lord, you are free to chose how that situation is to be handled. You can chose either to become angry or bitter and revengeful or you can chose to surrender yourself and the situation to Christ, making Him Lord in it all. You are free to chose never to stop allowing your body to be the channel through which the Lord Jesus can love the individual who has caused so much distress. The moment such a choice is made, you begin to experience what the Lord Jesus meant when He said, *"If you continue in My word, then you are truly disciples of Mine; and you will know the truth, and the truth will make you free…Truly, truly, I say to you, everyone who commits sin is the slave of sin…So if the Son makes you free, you will be free indeed"* (John 8:31-36).

The life which is surrendered to Christ is totally free in Him; free never to become embittered or overcome by hateful anger. Every challenge is now seen as an opportunity and never a hindrance. Here we have the key to that often misapplied scripture, (Rom. 8:26-30). The context is the Holy Spirit's present ministry interceding for God's people with God's purpose of each one becoming more like Christ very much in view. This is all wonderfully possible because our position in Christ means we are already glorified.

*"In the same way the Holy Spirit also helps our weakness; for we do not know how to pray as we should, but the Spirit Himself intercedes for us with groanings too deep for words; and He who searches the hearts knows what the mind of the Spirit is, because He intercedes for the saints **according to the will of God**. And we know that God causes all things to work together for good **to those who love God, to those who are called according to His purpose**. For those whom He foreknew, He also predestined **to become conformed to the image of His Son**, so that He would be the firstborn among many brethren; and these whom He predestined, He also called; and these whom He called, He also justified; and these whom He justified, **He also glorified"** (Rom. 8:26-30).*

I urge you to take time to quietly and prayerfully think this through because this is real freedom, the kind of thing today's broken world knows nothing about. The individual who, day by day and constantly throughout each day is surrendered to Christ as Lord walks in joyful, peaceful victory. Each challenge is an opportunity to prove the reality of Christ loving through that individual. As you allow your God given imagination free rein you cannot help being deeply affected by the thought of all this could mean in today's churches. We are not talking about some warm fuzzy feeling but about love that is radical; love like no other; powerful, life transforming love; God's love.

The late Robert Chapman who, for many years, cared for the people in his local church in Barnstaple, Devon, England knew the meaning and power of God's radical love in his life and ministry. When someone came to him complaining about some very awkward individual in the church, someone who was upsetting all kinds of people. Some quiet words of wisdom from Mr. Chapman encouraged the complainer to turn his perception of the situation on its head. *"A very valuable brother that. We never knew how much we were in need of patience until he came among us."*

This is a glowing example of the radical love of God which transforms both parties in a situation like nothing else can.

Just how radical is this love we are talking about? Verses 8 and 9 of 1st Peter 4 use some pretty powerful language to describe it. First of all there is nothing more important; *"above all keep fervent in your love for one another."* This word "fervent" literally means to be stretched out; we might say, to the max. The same thought is in 1 Peter 1:22, *"since you have in obedience to the truth purified your souls for a sincere love of the brethren, **fervently love one another from the heart."***

In other words no other quality of love is ever envisaged among people who are in relationship with God through Christ. Nothing is more important. This gives added meaning to Jesus reply to Peter's question in Matthew 18:21-22; *"Lord, how often shall my brother sin against me and I forgive him? Up to seven times? Jesus said to him, I do not say to you up to seven times, but up to seventy times seven."*

It is easy to see that such a standard is totally impossible apart from the power of the Holy Spirit living in the individual.

Without too much thought I, and probably you too, can think of many people who are neither part of a local church nor are they walking with the Lord because some professing Christian has hurt them deeply. Such hurts can be well nigh completely destructive and some people carry them in their hearts for many years. One of the reasons for writing this book is to tell you that such a situation does not have to continue for one moment longer. Remember, we are free in Christ. Free to choose. Free to choose to surrender our will to the control of the Holy Spirit, thus allowing Him to change our heart attitude. Surrendering is very different to committing. You and I can commit to changing all we like but because, in ourselves we do not have what it takes to deal with such deep hurt, it will continue to drag us down and keep us in defeat. My heart has to be surrendered to the control of another; the Lord Jesus Christ. As a good friend of mine has pointed out, the response of someone being held up at gun point is never "I commit." Such a person is not in control of the situation. The terrified response would rather be "I surrender."

Someone known to me was deeply hurt years ago because of misguided actions taken by someone else; actions which were potentially ruinous. The entire situation was prayed over. Wise counsel was obtained and the whole matter surrendered to the Lord Jesus. There was no gossip or thoughts of revenge. It took some years but eventually the individual was completely vindicated and a beautiful reconciliation took place which resulted in the re-establishing of a loving friendship in the Lord.

Without doubt this quality of love is foreign to our sad and broken world. This is radical love because it is the reproduction in a human heart of God's own love. The word used for love in the original language is *agape*, described in Vine's Expository Dictionary of New Testament Words as "the characteristic word of Christianity." It is obvious from its use in the New Testament that behind this word is a totally unique concept. Going back to Peter's use of the word we discover that believers in the Lord Jesus have the resources to be able to get rid of all hindrances to such love operating among them so that they can *"fervently love one another from the heart."* They have those resources on the basis of having been *"born again."* The context of those words is interesting (1 Pet. 1:21-23). God has raised the Lord Jesus from the dead and He is now exalted in the glory of heaven. Without this we as Christians have nothing. The historic, bodily, resurrection of Jesus Christ from the dead is God's vindication of who He is and of the eternal significance of what He accomplished through His death on the cross (Rom. 1:1-4). In no sense therefore are our "faith and hope" either misplaced or misguided. Both are in God who is *"from everlasting to everlasting"* (Ps. 90:2), *"creator of the ends of the earth"* (Isa. 40:28), *"the God of Abraham, the God of Isaac and the God of Jacob"* (Ex. 3:6), *"the God and Father of our Lord Jesus Christ"* (Eph. 1:3) and, as Jesus Himself said, *"My Father and your Father, My God and your God"* (John 20:17). All this gives such rich meaning to Peter's description of what it means to be *"born again."* It means so much more than simply being *"believers in God."* After all, as James tells us, *"the demons also believe and shudder"* (Jas. 2:19). Just as a series of photographs can depict different aspects of the same object or incident so

Peter indicates aspects of being born again which demonstrate the radical nature of the love he is talking about.

Aspect 1 *"obedience to the truth"* - Some people have a problem with the concept of absolute truth. They become rather upset with Christians in particular who make truth claims. It has been well said that to say there is no absolute truth is illogical. Making such a statement is in itself a claim to absolute truth. Imagine the chaos if it were discovered that 1+1=2 is no longer absolutely true. When Jesus claims to be **"the truth"** (John 14:6) and when Peter speaks in this text about "obedience to **the truth"** (1 Pet. 1:22) the Greek word, *aletheia*, is used in the sense of divine truth revealed to man. In the context of claiming to be the truth Jesus says, *"he who has seen Me has seen the Father"* (John 14:9). In other words the absolute truth, almighty God Himself, is revealed in Jesus. It is impossible to honestly examine all we know of the historical Jesus, His birth, His life, His death, His resurrection, His ascension and to come to any other conclusion. He is the revelation of God to man. He is **"the truth."** The Greek word for obedience, hupakoe, literally means submission to what is heard. The only response to make to the truth which has been revealed in the Lord Jesus and proclaimed in the gospel is to submit to His authority in my life. Then, our *"faith and hope are in God"* (1 Pet. 1:21).

Aspect 2 It is impossible to submit to the truth and our lives not to be radically affected. That act of submission means I am putting from my life every known trace of impurity. Notice this scripture speaks about purifying our *"souls."* It is referring to our deep inner being, our real self. This gives added meaning to the expression, *"for you have been born again..."* (verse 23). Being born again is not a religious experience; there is nothing shallow about it. It means a totally transforming transaction between the soul and almighty God. It results in purification at the very core of our being.

Aspect 3 Our hearts are now clean. For the first time we have the indwelling resources to be able to *"fervently love one another from the heart"* (1 Pet. 1:22). Really grasping the full extent to which being born again completely transforms the life ought to make us take another look at our "reasons" for not being part of a local church. If we are currently members of a local church we ought to take another look at how the current state of our hearts is affecting our brothers and sisters in the church. It also should make us examine our past dealings with people who may not now be part of our local church. Did we contribute in any way to their present situation?

All that need concern you is, are you truly born again? Are you enjoying the deep inner soul cleanness that only the application of the blood of Christ through repentance and faith can make possible? Are you truly allowing the Lord Jesus to so fill you with His life that you are aware of His love flowing through you? Whatever response you may receive from the other person is not your problem, provided you have dealt with any root cause which is troubling your conscience. Agape love is a "no matter what" kind of love. It is never conditional on being loved in return. It is *"fervent"* and *"from the heart"* (1 Pet. 1:22).

Looking back now I can tell you that the highest point in my life was my lowest point. I will always be grateful to God the Holy Spirit who, when I was totally overwhelmed with discouragement, when there was massive temptation and I was on the verge of ruining my whole life, showed me the awful rottenness of my heart. I saw then that my heart was basically so sinful I was capable of just about anything. The memory of that day in my little study is so vivid; broken and deeply repentant, I surrendered the whole dreadful mess together with all of my innermost being to the Lord Jesus. I was a Christian but had a deep lesson to learn about the surrendered life. It dawned on me that the secret of ongoing victory lay in total surrender to Christ as Lord and in allowing Him to live His life in and through me every moment of every day. This is something I had known in my head for years. Now it was reaching my heart. Deep and terrible as it was I would not have missed that experience for the world. Like you, I am so grateful for people like my wife and family, who know me best and yet still love me. I'm grateful too for dear brothers and sisters in the body of Christ who love me by God's grace. But it doesn't really matter whether everybody loves me or not. God loves me and, because He led me as a born again Christian to a new understanding of complete surrender to Jesus as Lord, *"the love of God has been poured out within [my] heart through the Holy Spirit who was given to [me]"* (Rom. 5:5). When there are situations where, for whatever reason, people don't love me, the situation can now be surrendered to the Lordship of Christ so He can love through me. Praise His wonderful name.

It is so important to have the Lord's own perspective on this matter of radical love. In His high priestly prayer in John chapter 17 Jesus made this powerful statement which ought to cause us all to humble ourselves in repentance. Allow the words of Jesus to sink into your heart today:

*"I do not ask on behalf of these alone, **but for those also who believe in me through their word;** that they may all be one; even as You, Father, are in Me and I in You, that they also may be in Us, **so that the world may believe that you sent Me"** (John 17:20-21).

In other words the lack of this radical, supernatural love in the church, particularly in the Western world is probably the biggest single hindrance to people coming to know the Lord.

Challenge

Are you aware of resentment in your heart and, as a result, the inability to love some people? Then don't just pray some little prayer. Get before God and ask Him to really show you the awful sinfulness of your heart of which the lack of love is but a symptom. Stay there till that happens and you are willing to surrender your whole self to Christ as Lord in your life. Only this course of action by individuals will transform our local churches making them living proof of the reality of agape love.

SEVEN

Such Love is Powerful

If you are anything like me you will be realizing that the standards set in the New Testament regarding Christians loving one another are impossible. I have news for you; you are absolutely right. Not only are you right but you have just made the most momentous discovery you will ever make as a disciple of the Lord Jesus. This is where our thinking as Christians is raised to a whole new level. If it is impossible for me to love my brothers and sisters in Christ as God desires, what on earth is the point? The point is simply this; God, by His amazing grace, has called you to Himself. He has called you out of the world to be part of His Church. It is because the clear distinction between the church and the world has become so blurred that we have a problem grasping this concept. Because we have allowed ourselves to become contaminated by the low moral standards of the world we no longer have a clear understanding of what it means to be holy. The phrase, "in the world but not of the world," is bandied about as if it were the panacea for all our ills. The trouble is most of us put the emphasis on "in the world" rather than on "not of the world." Yes, Jesus received sinners and ate with them but never to the extent of compromise with their standards and ways.

Not only does our thinking need to be raised to a whole new level, but that must happen by one of the most fundamental truths of our faith being revealed to us. I know of a Bible study group where the majority of those attending, although they professed to be Christians, did not believe they were holy even though Paul addressed the members of all the churches to whom he wrote as "saints." Most of us, at some stage in our lives, are afflicted by the kind of false humility which really is a huge barrier to our understanding who we are in Christ. Oh! I'm no saint, we say when all the time God is trying to tell us that is exactly what we are. Allow me to go over some things again. In Galatians 6:14 the great apostle Paul says, *"but may it never be that I should boast, except in the cross of our Lord Jesus Christ, through which **the world has been crucified to me and I to the world.**"*

He is saying that, for him, the cross marks the spot where everything changed. When he came to the cross deeply convicted of how sinful he was in God's sight, he realized the significance of what Jesus did through His death on that cross. This was the only means by which he could be forgiven and begin a new life. At that moment for Paul, as he himself said when writing to the church in Corinth, *"the old things passed away; behold, new things have come"* (2 Cor. 5:17). His old life was now being left behind and a new one was beginning. It was a complete turn around, the very essence of genuine repentance. That moment of coming to the cross in repentance and faith meant the world and its sinful ways was being left behind. His life now took a new direction and had a new focus. Paul had come to the cross, been reconciled to God and was now moving on with the cross behind him. If Paul ever wore a cross around his neck, he probably would not wear it on his chest but hanging down his back!

Paul's experience of the cross is precisely that of every true believer in the Lord Jesus. Only by revelation can the significance of it come home to our hearts. God has done something in our lives which we could never do for ourselves. God has made us what we could never make ourselves. **He has made us holy**. It was Dr. Charles Feinberg who pointed out that the teaching of all religions is, "we do in order to become," whereas the teaching of Christianity is, "we become in order to do." The life of holiness is totally impossible without first being made holy. God wants you and I to understand and grasp the fact that, having turned from our sin and surrendered to Christ as Saviour and Lord, **He has made us holy.**

This is what banishes forever, to the realm of the ridiculous, the whole notion that the Christian life can be lived in isolation and not in the context of an expression of the body of Christ, a local church. The picture given in the New Testament is of the Universal Church with the Local Church being a part of it. There is a beautiful picture of the Universal Church in Ephesians chapter 4 where, having made a plea for walking *"in a manner worthy of the calling with which you have been called, with all humility and gentleness, with patience, showing tolerance for one another in love, being diligent to preserve the unity of the Spirit in the bond of peace"*, he goes on to say, **"there is one body and one Spirit..."** But this is written in the context of a letter to a Local Church, *"to the saints who are at Ephesus"* (Eph. 1:1). Were you to attend the famous Keswick Convention, held annually, in England's magnificent Lake District, you would see, above the entrance as you approached the huge tent where the main meetings are held, a quotation from Galatians chapter 6 verse 28, *"All one in Christ Jesus."* The convention is a beautiful expression of the Universal Church. However, when you get inside the tent you would soon realize that the thousands of people there represent a great variety of local churches. The people have come from churches all over the UK and indeed all over the world. Prof. E. P. Clowney writes, "the church may be defined as local, so that only the local church is the church proper and broader gatherings can be only associations of churches or of Christians. On the other hand, the church may be defined as universal, so that the local church is only a portion of the church, a part of the whole."[9]

The expression in Ephesians 4, *"there is one body"*, is highly significant. The word "church" is derived from the Greek word *ekklesia* (phonetically spelled, ek-klay-see'-ah). This word "mostly designates a local congregation of Christians and never a building. Although we often speak of these congregations collectively as the New Testament church or the early church, no New Testament writer uses *ekklesia* in this collective way. An *ekklesia* was a meeting or assembly."[10] This word *ekklesia* is from two root words, *ek*, meaning out from and to and *kaleo*, meaning to call.

---

9   Prof. E. P. Clowney, *New Dictionary of Theology*, IVP, 1988, page 141
10   Bishop D. W. B. Robinson, M.A., *The Illustrated Bible Dictionary*, IVP, 1980, page 283

Therefore the church is made up of people called out from the world and to God. In Ephesians chapter 1 verses 22 and 23 Paul describes the church as *"the church which is His body."* We can see then that knowing Christ as Saviour and Lord means belonging to the church which means belonging to His body which means we are part of Him. Ephesians 1:22 and 23 again, *"...and gave Him as head over all things to the church, which is His body, the fulness of Him who fills all in all."* Dear reader, I beg you to take time to think about this. It will be life changing as far as your concept of church is concerned and it will completely revolutionize your view of how you relate to your brothers and sisters in Christ. If you are part of that called out, called to, group of people you are part of Christ's body. You are a member of Christ. Just as no member of your physical body can function in isolation no more can you as a member of Christ's body. You can only function as a member of that body because life, His life, is flowing through you. I recently heard my nephew Andrew illustrate this point by showing that we, as Christians, do not have a kind of energizer battery inside us; "we have the whole national grid." The Lord Jesus does not give us little parcels of life, He gives us Himself. It is the living Christ Himself who resides on the inside of each child of God. That is why the kind of love we are talking about is powerful. Allow this truth to penetrate your mind and heart. All of us who are members of Christ's body are *"saints by calling"* (1 Cor. 1:2). New Testament words like, "saints", "holy", "sanctify", are all from the same Greek root, *hagios.* Look again at 1 Corinthians 1 verse 2, *"To the church of God which is at Corinth, to those who have been sanctified in Christ Jesus, saints by calling, with all who in every place call on the name of the Lord Jesus Christ, their Lord and ours."* All those words are combined in this verse to demonstrate that if you belong to the Lord **He has made you holy, He has sanctified you and therefore you are a saint.** The question is, are you and I going to continue to insult the Lord with our false humility, Oh, I'm no saint? Such an attitude really is the worst form of pride. Or are we going to take the Lord at His word, lose sight of ourselves all together and rejoice that He has already made us holy? Then as we surrender ourselves to Him every moment of every day His Holy life and love will flow through us.

As we now relate all this to the practical realities of church life we will begin to see just how powerful the love of God in each of us can be. If we are honest many of the people who are not really plugged in to a local church, who have either opted out all together or are taking the constant church hopping route, have good reason for so doing. We could say they have good reason only when we view the situation from a human perspective. The whole point of allowing the thrilling alternatives mentioned above to penetrate our minds and hearts is that we will see the entire situation through different eyes. We will see it from God's perspective. It is absolutely essential that this happen. Otherwise nothing will ever change. To illustrate what I mean, a careful reading of Paul's letter to the church at Colosse will demonstrate how we ought to be viewing our local church. Just imagine the letter was written, not to the church at Colosse but to *"saints and faithful brethren who are at* _____ *"* Insert the name of your local community there.

When you have a truly biblical view of your local church you will never become simply parochial in your outlook. One of the main reasons for people becoming discontented and judgmental in their local church is that their vision is far too small. In chapter one of Colossians Paul encourages them in their *"faith in Christ Jesus and the love which [they] have for all the saints"* (v. 4). He then lifts their minds above their current circumstances to *"the hope laid up for [them] in heaven."* All of this, he reminds them, is because of *"the word of truth, the gospel."* Not only does he lift their minds to things above but he broadens their vision to take in the entire world. Every Christian ought to have a biblical WORLD view; *"...the gospel which has come to you, **just as in all the world also it is constantly bearing fruit and increasing"*** (1:6). If you want to encourage yourself and others in your local church make it your business to gather information about the amazing ways the gospel is "bearing fruit and increasing" world wide. Our western society is no longer the hub of things as far as church growth is concerned. The growth of the church in China, Asia, South America and the Middle East is thrilling. Those are the missionary sending nations in today's world.

Think of how those boring church prayer meetings could be revolutionized were they to be based on chapter one verses 9-14! This is the kind of praying that comes from hearts filled with all the resources of the "national grid" of God's life and power flowing through them. Such saints are praying for one another that each would be *"filled with the knowledge of His will in all spiritual wisdom and understanding, so that you will walk in a manner worthy of the Lord, **to please Him in all respects**, bearing fruit in every good work and increasing in the knowledge of God; strengthened with all power, **according to His glorious might**, for the attaining of all steadfastness and patience, **joyously giving thanks** to the Father, who has qualified us to share in the inheritance of the saints in light."*

So why are our prayer meetings or, for that matter, most of our local church activities, not dominated by that kind of godly spirit? It is because we have failed to really understand the extent to which our "flesh" is in control. Paul said, "for I know that nothing good dwells in me, that is, in my flesh..." (Rom. 7:18). Looking back over the more than four decades my wife and I have been in ministry, the times of which I am most ashamed are the times when my fleshly nature was allowed to be dominant. Those were the times when my attitude was all wrong, when I have used words which I now deeply regret. They were the times when, although being hit by circumstances over which I had no control, I became introverted instead of opening it all up to the Lord, allowing Him to take control of my thought life. The results sometimes came pretty close to being disastrous. Only by the grace of God am I sitting here right now writing this manuscript, filled with the deepest joy and gratitude. If there is one thing for which I'm grateful to God, far and away above everything else in my life as a Christian, it is for the times when God brought me to a Peter like experience (see Luke 22:54-62). Like Peter, I was so ashamed of my weakness, pride and self-centeredness that I wept bitterly. Today I know, beyond all doubt, that the only way to deal with my fleshly nature is to understand with Paul that *"I have been crucified with Christ: and that **it is no longer I who live, but Christ lives in me...**"* (Gal. 2:20).

At the risk of laboring the point may I illustrate it further? I'm praying that as you read this you, with me, will be totally honest as you examine the situation. Our local churches are so divided, fragmented and weak because there is so little repentance over the way we have allowed our fleshly natures to have the upper hand. There is a very interesting phrase in Exodus 17:8. The people of Israel, under the leadership of Moses, had seen God do some amazing things. Then, right out of the blue we are told, *"then Amalek came and fought against Israel at Rephidim."* We have to go back to Genesis 36:12, 16 to discover Amalek's beginnings. There we are told he was the grandson of Esau and Esau, Jacob's brother, sold his inheritance for a bowl of some kind of stew. Amalek is therefore descended from this one who exhibited a total disregard for his birthright. In fact scripture tells us that he *"despised his birthright"* (Gen. 25:34), a step he later bitterly regretted. The hatred for Jacob's descendants had, no doubt, been inbred in Amalek and nurtured in his heart with the passage of time. Amelek showed up at various stages in Israel's journey to the land God had promised them when He said, *"And I am come down to deliver them out of the hand of the Egyptians, and to bring them up out of that land unto a good land and a large, unto a land flowing with milk and honey"* (Ex. 3:8). When Amalek appears on the scene his objective was to hinder the progress of God's people in their journey to the land God had promised them. For that reason Amalek is often thought of as a picture of our fleshly nature. It is always there and, all of us, if we are honest, have to admit that this is where the vast majority of our problems as Christians come from. Some of us want to blame the devil for stuff he has nothing to do with. Most of our problems come from our selfish, sinful, fleshly nature. The Bible is very clear as to how Moses dealt with Amalek. There was no question of the problem being tackled only by putting up a fight. It was important for the people to stand against Amalek (Ex. 17:9a). But it was even more important that Moses, with *"the staff of God in* [his] *hand"* would stand on top of the mountain holding the staff high thus depicting God's absolute supremacy over Amalek. The *"staff of God"* was carried by Moses throughout the desert journey and was the symbol of God's power on behalf of His people. So long as Moses arms were raised holding the staff Israel was winning. But as soon as the staff was lowered, Amalek was winning. There is such an important lesson to be learned here. When Moses grew tired and allowed his arms to fall the enemy began to take over. The answer? Aaron and Hur supported Moses in every way possible for as long as it took. Yes, there is a battle to be fought but it is also a battle to be won. It will only be won when the main focus is on the power of God pictured in the staff being held high. Had it been left to Moses alone Amalek would probably have prevailed but he had the support of his colleagues, Aaron and Hur. There is no doubt "Amalek" is having a field day in the 21st century western church. **You and I cannot go it alone.** We each need the support and fellowship or our fellow believers. There are therefore some clear steps to victory over Amalek in our lives and in our churches. These are steps to be taken because of a deep awareness of the weakness of our fleshly nature.

1. Each one unconditionally surrendered to the Lordship of Jesus Christ in his or her life.

2. Each one thoroughly committed to the local church; that part of Christ's body to which each belongs

3. Each one therefore allowing the powerful love of Christ to flow through them to their brothers and sisters in the local church.

4. Each one therefore with the vision to pray for the others in prevailing prayer.

The end result, "Amalek" is "overwhelmed."

Going back to Colossians again and reading this time in chapter two, we discover at least three principles which help us to understand just how powerful God's love can be in the relationships between Christians. It is important to understand that the concepts taught in the New Testament are addressed to people who had much more of a community mind set than the individualistic mind set of our western society. In other words the New Testament believers thought much more corporately than we do. They did not come at everything in life with a consumer attitude. They understood they were part of each other and that each one had a responsibility to contribute to the life of the local church (something we will look at in more detail later). They were not

looking for what the church had to offer them. The three principles I'm suggesting Paul taught the Christians at Colosse as being
essential to their spiritual health and wellbeing are:

There were clear **priorities** affecting their relationships with
one another:

I am well aware that your life may be exceedingly busy.
Or not so much busy, just a never ending cycle of things going
wrong in your family, work or finances. For you its true, "reality
spoils life." You may have little idea, if any, what other people
could possibly have to do with you or you with them. Right
now you simply can't cope with "fellowship" in any shape or
form. In fact if you are attending a church at all, it may be very
reluctantly, and on many Sunday mornings you would much
rather stay home. After all some of the best Bible teaching available can be heard by switching on the TV. Its tempting to sit in
your PJ's, hugging a cup of coffee, while you get your spiritual
shot for another week. Believe me, that is exactly where many
people are today. Not only is it very sad but, if the motivation
behind it is wrong, for whatever reason, it is deeply grieving to
the Holy Spirit. Praise God for the quality of teaching on many
of today's TV channels. Such teaching is meeting needs and
leading many to Christ but it is not a viable substitute for being
actively involved in a local church.

Have you ever thought about your local church in terms
of the priorities taught in Colossians chapter 2? Bear in mind
that any church lacking in them is dysfunctional. So important were they that Paul spoke of "struggling" on their behalf,
longing that such priorities would not just be theory but reality among the Christians to whom he wrote. The priorities as
Paul saw them are:

1. That encouragement would come from the realization
that their hearts were *"knit together in love."*

It is interesting to see that he does not pray for this as though
it were something yet to be achieved. He rather prayed that
their hearts would be encouraged, *"having been knit together in
love."* It is rather a question of discovering experientially what is
already an accomplished fact because: there is immense wealth

to be enjoyed. All we need is already ours. It is just a question of coming to *"full assurance of understanding."* This is not merely a matter of the intellect, it is a matter of great truth reaching the heart through revelation to the mind. *"God's mystery"* is not knowledge withheld, it is rather truth revealed. The ultimate revelation of God and His truth is Christ Himself, *"in whom are hidden all the treasures of wisdom and knowledge"* (v. 3). In other words, what Paul is saying, is that as Christians they are in Christ so they have everything they need for this immensely powerful love of God to be released through them to one another.

2. They were left in no doubt as to where the **power** to maintain those relationships was to come from.

It was directly related to the *"stability of [their] faith in Christ"* (Col. 2:5). This was the key to progress in their "walk in Him" (v. 6). Bear in mind that this was at the very heart of all that gave Paul cause to thank God each time he thought about the Christians at Colosse, *"we give thanks to God the Father of our Lord Jesus Christ, praying always for you since we heard of your faith in Christ Jesus and the love which you have for all the saints"* (Col. 1:3-4). His encouragement to them now is, *"therefore, as you received Christ Jesus the Lord, so walk in Him"* (Col. 2:6). In other words that they keep growing in the life of faith. They were already *"firmly rooted"* the added challenge was of *"now being built up in Him and established in (or by) your faith"* (v. 7). The Colossian Christians were obviously well taught because Paul describes them as having been *"instructed."* More will also be said about this later, but for the moment suffice it to say that, in my experience, for most people who have trouble becoming planted in a local church, the lack of the kind of instruction which establishes and builds them up in their faith is the main problem. Receiving such instruction on a regular basis will produce the kind of Christians who are *"overflowing with gratitude."* Speaking personally, there is no doubt in my mind that, relative to my development in my walk of faith, nothing causes me to be more thankful than the thought of the instruction I received in my early years as a believer. My church leaders went to a great deal of trouble and effort to make sure the sheep for whom they were responsible before the Lord were fed a truly nourishing diet of spiritual food; the kind which *"built up and established."*

3. Christ was ever to be **preeminent** in all their thinking. It can never be emphasized too strongly that we are called, as Christians, to be disciples of the Lord Jesus. That means Jesus will "have first place in everything" (Col. 1:18). If He has first place in our lives then *"in Him [we] have been made complete"* (Col. 2:10). That has to mean that our world view has been radically altered. We no longer look at things from a consumerist's point of view; what's in it for me, but *"rather...according to Christ"* (v. 8). After all, *"in Him all the fulness of Deity dwells in bodily form, and in Him you have been made complete, and He is the head over all rule and authority....."* (v. 9-10). The wonderful thing about all of this is that we, who, before we met Christ, were spiritually "dead", are now *"alive together with Him."* "ALL our transgressions" have been forgiven. That means we are no longer under the condemnation of God's law (the ten commandments). Jesus took all the condemnation and judgement we deserved upon Himself when He died as our substitute on the cross. Really living this experientially will create within us a truly attractive holiness. All that will concern us will be that Christ have first place in our lives and that He therefore live His life in us and through us. Consider carefully the difference this would make if every member of your local church were enjoying Christ to that extent. Please don't make excuses now about my not knowing what its like in your church. That's true, but please bear in mind the teaching on prayer in the previous chapter.

With all this in mind there are no excuses now for either shallow or conditional love to exist among Christians. If it is the number one characteristic which distinguishes us as disciples of Christ (John 13:34-35) then the lack of love among us ought to appall us as nothing else will. The more I think of Peter's expression in 1 Peter 4:8, *"because love covers a multitude of sins,"* the more beautiful it becomes. Remember Peter is talking here about being "fervent" in loving one another. It literally means loving one another to the max. The beauty of this concept is in the fact that such love *"covers a multitude of sins."* The Greek word for covers is *kalupto* which means, "to hide" or "keep secret." In other words because I love my brother or sister in Christ *"fervently from the heart"* (1 Pet. 1:22) I will want to pray for them and have input into their lives so that no one else will ever become aware of their particular short coming. All the time I will be deeply aware of how glad I am that others are not aware of the shortcomings and sins in my own life.

I will never forget the shock of realizing my mother was afflicted with dementia and not just with the normal limitations of advancing years. I was not aware of her situation at all until my father passed away. His love for her meant there were no limits to the extent of his care. That kind of loving and selfless care hid and kept secret a problem which, I am sure, was affecting him and his quality of life considerably.

The kind of love God desires to reproduce in His people is *agape* (pronounced ag-ah-pay). This word refers to divine love and, speaking very practically, this love can be reproduced in our lives because Jesus, the perfect expression of this love, lives on the inside of us. Therefore the powerful words of 1 Corinthians 13:4-5 become gloriously possible; *"love is patient, love is kind, and is not jealous; love does not brag and is not arrogant, does not act unbecomingly; it does not seek its own, is not provoked, does not take into account a wrong suffered...."* We have an equally powerful description of this love in Ephesians 4:32; *"be kind to one another, tenderhearted, **forgiving each other, just as God in Christ also has forgiven you."***

Even as I write these lines I'm humbling myself in the presence of God, realizing how many times the Holy Spirit has been grieved in my own heart in this area. Yet, at the same time, I'm rejoicing in how freeing this whole concept is on realizing again that *"I have been crucified with Christ and it is no longer I who live, but Christ lives in me; and the life which I now live in the flesh I live by faith in the Son of God who loved me and gave Himself up for me"* (Gal. 2:20).

The extent to which we in today's church have lost the sense of wonder we ought to have as we think through such scripture passages is so sad. Even when, as can easily happen, a brother or sister in Christ is *"caught in any trespass"* (Gal. 6:1), people who are walking with God and in the wonder of His indwelling life, will have as their first concern to *"restore such a one in a spirit of gentleness; each one looking to* [themselves], *so that* [they] *too will not be tempted."*

I never want to forget the little ditty which says, "if everyone in my church were just like me, what kind of church would my church be?" It was the late David Watson who was Vicar of St. Michael le Belfrey, York, England who said, "Fellowship begins at our points of weakness and not at our points of strength." There is something so wonderful, so life changing and so church transforming about all this.

Challenge

Are you willing to take a humble and honest look at your own "points of weakness" with particular concern about how they are affecting your attitudes to and relations with your fellow believers? Is what you discover a factor in how you view the local church and does it have anything to do with why you may be reluctant to be part of one?

EIGHT

Such Love is Selfless

Whatever, *"be hospitable to one another without complaint"* (1 Pet. 4:9) might mean, it does not mean having your friends over for dinner; not in this context anyway. Opening our homes to friends can be a very effective avenue for sharing our faith and for deeper fellowship. However in the context of 1 Peter I believe it has to be seen more as a characteristic of the selfless caring which ought to be evident among God's people. The Greek word is *philoxenos* meaning hospitable or loving strangers. In other words being hospitable in this sense means blessing people we may never have met nor are likely to meet again. When we remember that most of the New Testament letters were written against a background of serious persecution, then hospitality takes on a whole new meaning. The very first verse of Peter's first letter tells us that he is writing to disciples of Christ who are widely scattered because of persecution. They had been called upon to be *"distressed by various trials"* (1:6). We, in our comfortable western situation, tend to forget that the majority of our brothers and sisters in Christ throughout the world are suffering serious persecution. For so many taking a stand for the Lord Jesus means losing their jobs, being disowned by their family and, in many cases, having to literally flee for their lives. Since the birth of the church in Acts chapter 2 God's people have had to suffer persecution. It is just as Jesus said it would be:

"If the world hates you, you know that it has hated Me before it hated you. If you were of the world, the world would love its own; but because you are not of the world, but I chose you out of the world, because of this the world hates you" (John 15:18-19).

This highlights for us one of the main reasons why we need one another so much. In a world like our's it is so wrong for any of us to imagine for a moment that we can operate independently. The persecuted church throughout the world ought to be a constant goad in our side, motivating us to constantly examine our priorities, all the time remembering that every persecuted saint throughout the world is our brother or sister in the Lord. You may well say, but I don't have to be part of a local church to be concerned for the persecuted church. While there may be an element of truth in that, the chances of an isolated Christian who is not enjoying stimulating fellowship with other believers and who is not being regularly taught from God's Word being aware of the scale of the world wide persecution are pretty slim.

In the end it all comes down to realizing that knowing Christ as Saviour and Lord automatically means belonging to a group of people, the Church, who are called out of the world and into relationship with the living God. We are now reconciled to God. The Church, His body is, as we have seen already, a "called out" people. Jesus Himself said, *"My kingdom is not of this world,"* meaning His kingdom was not from this world. This is why the New Testament lays such stress on radical holiness and the separated life.

In the days of the early church the believers were made scapegoats for the fire of Rome for example. They were looked upon as social misfits and anti-social; *"...they are surprised that you do not run with them into the same excess of dissipation, and they malign you"* (1 Pet. 4:4). *"if you are reviled for the name of Christ, you are blessed, because the Spirit of glory and of God rests on you"* (1 Pet. 4:14). I have had the great privilege of preaching in parts of the world where God's people are suffering greatly. Being with such believers made an indelible impression on me. In some places we were reminded that "walls have ears." In others just going for a walk meant being followed and watched constantly. I had one preaching engagement cancelled at the very last minute because under the circumstances of that particular day, if I had been seen going to the place of meeting it would have meant danger for the local believers, especially in the days following. In some places Christian children have seen their parents murdered before their eyes. In other cases parents had their children kidnapped or murdered or both.

I will never forget the time when four of us from the west met with two brothers in Christ for a prayer time. One of those men had been a believer for a few years and the other for only a few months. Both had been in prison for their faith several times. The prayer time was one of the most humbling and challenging experiences of my life. We prayed for a while and we westerners were so concerned to tell the Lord the things we had on our hearts. Our eastern brothers on the other hand had a completely different attitude in prayer. For example, after we had prayed for some time they turned to us asking us individually what the Lord had been saying to us during the prayer time. They understood that prayer was a two way exercise; talking to God and hearing from Him. They were men of the word. Being in constant communion with the Lord was their only source of strength and courage as they faced a very uncertain future.

I don't know about you, but when I think of those dear believers in Jesus I'm left with the distinct impression we are only playing at church here in the west. But it does not have to be like that. Such a sad situation need not continue for another moment. The choice is ours. You may be looking for a church where you can be comfortable and not have your nicely planned routine disturbed. All you may want is a group of Christians who share your values and who belong to a church with the kind of youth group which will keep your kids entertained and off the streets. Then I question whether you have ever understood what the church really is. One of the lasting impressions I have from my times with persecuted believers is that most of their young people are more mature spiritually than many of us who are in positions of leadership in western churches. Their walk with God is real and deep. Their prayer lives are passionate and vital. Their love for God's word can only be described as an insatiable hunger. They are bold in their witness and, in spite of all they have to suffer, their joy in the Lord is infectious. In short, it is an enormous privilege to spend even a short time in their godly company.

But we are only responsible for our situation here in the west, I hear you say. That is true to some extent but let me remind you, *"there is one body and one Spirit, just as you were called in one hope of your calling; one Lord, one faith, one baptism, one God and Father of all who is over all and through all and in all"* (Eph. 4:4-6). Therefore it has to be a mark of an alive and growing local church that we, the members, have a selfless love and care for those who are suffering because they love the Lord.

One thing that has moved me deeply over the years as I have travelled to various parts of the world is to see people who are by no means wealthy respond with amazing generosity to the needs of the suffering church. Although they may not be able to have hands-on involvement, they practiced hospitality by giving sacrificially of their personal resources. All it needed was for their hearts to be touched by the Holy Spirit as to the need and their hospitality was *"without complaint."* It was willing and from the heart. Such people are emulating the Macedonian Christians of whom we are told in 2 Corinthians chapter 8. Notice the stages leading up to their outpouring of love for their brothers and sisters who were suffering. Note the spiritual progression leading up to such an uncomplaining expression of godly hospitality.

Their generous giving was the product of *"the grace of God which [had] been given to the churches of Macedonia"* (v. 1).

Therefore their giving was with an *"abundance of joy"*, and it *"overflowed in the wealth of their liberality."* All this was in the face of *"a great ordeal of affliction....and deep poverty"* (v. 2).

How much they thought they could afford did not come into it. It was *"according to their ability, and beyond their ability, they gave of their own accord"* (v. 3).

They, the givers, enjoyed as much of the blessing as did the recipients; *"begging us with much urging **for the favor of participation in the support of the saints"*** (v. 4).

All this was the product of a simple yet profound principle, **"they first gave themselves to the Lord and to us by the will of God"** (v. 5).

Seeing verses of scripture in their biblical context is essential to a true and balanced understanding of their teaching and application. Take for example the oft quoted Proverbs 3:5-6. *"trust in the Lord with all your heart and do not lean on your own* *understanding. In **all** your ways acknowledge Him, and He will make your paths straight."* If I am to know what that means in real terms I need to go first to verse 1, *"my son, do not forget my teaching, but let your heart keep my commandments."* In other words, it begins with the surrender of my life to God resulting in submission to His word. Trusting Him will then take on a new meaning and will mean, among other things, that my material possessions will also be part of the surrender package. There will be no question; I will then *"honor the Lord from [my] wealth and from the first of all [my] produce"* (v. 9). There is no doubt verses 5 and 6 are foundational for life as they stand but in the wider context they are given another and more exciting dimension.

It is not unusual for us to focus on the promise of verse 10 when thinking about how we ought to handle our material possessions; *"so your barns will be filled with plenty and your vats will overflow with new wine."* It is an encouraging promise but homing on that aspect of things at the expense of the wider context brings into question our motivation in giving and robs us of so much joy in our giving; what I would call, Macedonian joy.

Some comments from the Rev. Derek Kidner in his commentary on the book of Proverbs will be helpful here.

> "We tend to seize on verse 10, either critically or hopefully. But it must not steal the thunder of verse 9. To know God in our financial 'ways' is to see that these *honor* Him; the honor will be compounded largely of homage (in giving Him the first and not a later share; compare 1 Cor. 16:2; Mark 12:44), of gratitude (see Deut. 26:9-11) and of trust (compare verse 5), for such giving in the face of material pressures is a simple test of faith. But a basic ingredient is fair business dealings; and this is saved up for fuller treatment in the final paragraph (v. 27-35).
>
> Verse 10. The generalization that piety brings *plenty* chimes in with much of Scripture (e.g. Deut. 28:1-14; Mal. 3:10) and of experience. If it were *more* than a

generalization… God would be not so much hon-
ored, as invested in, by our gifts…"[11]

It is a mark of a healthy church when a large portion of their
budget is set aside for giving to Missions, especially the kind of
giving that could be described as showing "hospitality" to the
suffering church throughout the world. It is rather sad when
cuts are being made in budget figures, the thing that is first to
go is this *hospitality giving*. It is an enduring biblical principle
that giving is, first of all, from surrendered hearts. It is therefore
willing and sacrificial, generous and joyful. Such giving will
bring great glory to the Lord and blessing to those who give.
This is something every Christian can do, whether rich or poor,
with the same joyous reward as was experienced in Macedonia.
It has been rightly said, "God is no man's debtor."

Even as I have been working on this book, having felt the
Lord's leading to give quality time to this writing, a substan-
tial gift to our ministry came in today's mail. I'm rejoicing in
God's faithfulness. Giving that is truly instigated by the Holy
Spirit creates an all round joy as giver and recipient rejoice in
the goodness of God.

All this is intensely practical and yet it will be the natural overflow from hearts where Jesus Christ truly is Lord.
Everything, including our financial resources will be surrendered to Him. Hear the word from 1 John 3:16-18, *"We know love
by this, that He laid down His life for us; and we ought to lay down
our lives for the brethren. But whoever has this worlds goods and sees
his brother in need and closes his heart against him, how does the love
of God abide in him? Little children, let us not love with word or with
tongue, but in deed and truth."*

Yes, you could do this to a certain extent without being
part of a local church. But Paul's instructions in 1 Corinthians
16 leave us in no doubt they were given in the context of the
church at Corinth and that church's giving to their brothers and
sisters in Jerusalem who were in real need.

---

11   Rev. Derek Kidner, M.A.; *The Proverbs: An Introduction and Commentary;* The
Tyndale Press; page 64

Challenge

So the local church you are looking for ought to be one which practices love that is selfless. And, even if such a place is hard to find, test your own heart in this area. Is Jesus Lord of your bank account? Be faithful to the Lord in this area of your life and don't allow anything to rob you of the joy which can be yours. Be a Macedonian type Christian.

SECTION 3

I Need A Church

Because it is where God can make me most effective
in making a difference
1 Peter 4:10

Something to think about...

It is a well known statistic that in most churches 80% of the work is done by 20% of the people. Therefore it is not rocket science to work out that 80% of people in local churches are missing out on one of the most important reasons for being there. A huge contributor to the spiritual growth of any Christian is their knowing and using the spiritual gift or gifts God has given them. The local church is the context God has designed for this to happen.

You may think you can use your gift without being part of a church. But that would be like your arm deciding it no longer wanted to be part of your body because it would much rather function on its own. You must never forget that being a Christian means being in a meaningful relationship with the living Lord Jesus. It is in such a relationship that you are literally part of Him, part of His body. The body is the picture used in the New Testament to describe the church. In that body He is the head and each believer is a member. Therefore it is impossible for any member to function effectively while physically separated from the rest of the body.

In this section I hope to show conclusively that the New Testament consistently envisages the local church as being a vehicle for good and for the glory of God in any given community. A vehicle in which,

THERE ARE NO PASSENGERS.

NINE

I'm Called to do Something

Unbelief, false humility and disobedience, in that order, are the root causes why there is so much latent gifting in the church. Unbelief, even though God's word clearly says, *"as **each one** has received a special gift..."* So many of us simply refuse to believe that. Since walking by faith is basic to growing in the Lord, not taking God at His word when He says each of us has a gift, results in the Holy Spirit being grieved in our lives. Think what you are missing in the way of personal enrichment and effectiveness if this is true of you. An attitude of unbelief is very often covered over by false humility; "Oh! I'm not very gifted, God could never use me." That is nothing other than the language of false humility because God tells you so that, if you are a child of God through faith in the Lord Jesus Christ, you are *"a new creature."* You are no longer the person you once were. You have been changed from the inside out. Christ lives on the inside of you by the Holy Spirit and remember, your gifting is the result of His life in you. A gift, by the very nature of things, has nothing whatever to do with you or me, it is something we have received from Him Who has come to take up residence within us. *"But one and the same Spirit works all these things, distributing to **each one** individually just as He wills"* (1 Cor. 12:11). This is so important. We all need to be challenged deeply in this area. If my attitude today is one of unbelief and false humility then I am being down right disobedient. I am selfishly refusing to use the gifting God has given me, *"for the common good"* (1 Cor. 12:7). If you read that verse you will see it is in the context again of the body of Christ with each member functioning as God ordained it should.

The various passages in the New Testament giving us teaching about gifts all emphasize certain basic tenets. The gifts operate in the context of Christ's body and so contribute to the health and well being of the body. Each member operates in his or her area of gifting according to directions from Christ, Who is the head. Secondly, when God given gifts are being used effectively it is always in an atmosphere of love; agape or divine love. And thirdly, the gifts operate in the context of the local church. See 1 Corinthians chapters 12, 13 and 14.

In Romans 12 it is evident that the gifts are as varied as are the people in the local church. No one individual has all the gifts; not even the pastor. Some pastors think they do and that is why they are suffering burn out in so many cases. More time needs to be spent *"equipping"* God's people. More of that later. Verses 6-10 of Romans 12 demonstrate the wide sweep of gifting the Lord has implanted in His body. Some are public and visible, some are quieter and often unseen. Others are intensely practical and at the same time fraught with temptations unless handled by people who are truly gifted in them; things like giving or leadership. Giving is something we are all challenged to do, *"on the first day of every week **each one of you** is to put aside and save, as he may prosper, so that no collections be made when I come"* (1 Cor. 16:2). But some are especially gifted in the handling of money and that is why it is singled out as a gift in Romans 12:8. Leadership is the ability to see what needs to be done and then to get on with it. In the wrong hands this can degenerate into manipulation or control or it can be selfishly motivated by a desire for *"sordid gain"* or a to be *"lording it over"* God's people (1 Pet. 5:2-3).

Ephesians 4 gives a different picture as far as gifts are concerned. There the risen Lord Jesus gives certain people as gifts to the church. They are, *"some as apostles, and some as prophets, and some as evangelists, and some as pastors and teachers"* (v. 11). The next verse makes it clear why those individuals are given as gifts to God's people. They are given *"for the **equipping of the saints** for the work of service, to the building up of the body of Christ."* Nowhere in the New Testament is a situation ever envisaged where one individual does it all. Those gifts to the church are there so that they will equip the members of the body to be able, in their turn, to use their own gifts so as to contribute to the building up of others. After all the end result in view is, *"until we all attain to the unity of the faith, and of the knowledge of the Son of God, to a mature man, to the measure of the stature which belongs to the fulness of Christ"* (v. 13).

It was such a freeing thing for me when it was made clear that the gifting God has given me is not a matter either of my own desire or a figment of my imagination. By God's grace I am gifted as an evangelist and in teaching God's word as an exhorter. Sensing this to be the case as a young man, confirmation came when I shared my thoughts on the matter with my church leadership only to discover that it came as no surprise to them. So much so that they were willing to recognize and support me in those areas. Even to this day I receive confirmation from people whom I recognize as my accountability structure. Another important area of confirmation is that people do come to faith in Christ as I function as an evangelist. Also the lives of many people who already know the Lord are stimulated in the area of spiritual growth through exhortation from God's word.

If you are not part of a local body of Christians or if you are having difficulties with the whole idea, I trust you are beginning to understand what you are missing out on. You are gifted and your gifts are essential to the growth of the church in your community. Do not believe any lie to the contrary. Allow yourself to be challenged and seriously think this one through. As you read on it is my prayer that you will first of all be willing to be available to the Lord in your area of gifting. And, secondly, you will be teachable as we outline more of why this is important and how you can know what your gifting is.

1 Peter 4:10 and, as we shall see later, verse 11 make it clear there is an important job to be done. So important that we are lifted far above anything that could be described as mundane. We are left in no doubt that there is absolutely no room whatever for seeking position, power or personal gain. The whole matter begins with the grace of God and the end result is *"that God may be glorified through Jesus Christ, to whom belongs the glory and dominion for ever and ever."* In other words there is no room whatsoever for self. A John the baptist attitude is

called for, *"He must increase but I must decrease"* (John 3:30). Paul never lost sight of this great principle either, *"...it is no longer I who live, but Christ lives in me..."* (Gal. 2:20).

There is little doubt that in the New Testament the local church is God's chosen means of fulfilling His purposes in the world. Each church is meant to be the place where God's people in any given community are being strengthened in their faith. This happens when, as they did in the early church, they *"continue devoting [ourselves] to the apostles teaching and to fellowship, to the breaking of bread and to prayer"* (Acts 2:42). Spiritual growth is stunted if any one of those four components is either missing or being neglected. Again it must be emphasized those things cannot contribute to spiritual growth anywhere else other than in the local church. This is the place where the word of God ought to be taught as food for the souls of God's people. It is the place where encouraging fellowship ought to be experienced. We all take a battering from the world as we deal with the harsh realities of daily life. Fellowship in our local church ought to provide healing and renewal. Keeping near the cross, being at the very heart of our faith, happens when we regularly remember the Lord Jesus by taking bread and wine, the symbols of Christ's broken body and poured out blood. Any Christian who is not regularly remembering the Lord Jesus in this way in the context of the local church is being disobedient. If we are honest we will all readily acknowledge that, while praying alone is essential, it is very difficult to maintain over time. A reading of the New Testament makes clear that there was great power in the ministry and witness of the early church because they were constantly praying together.

Being aware of the history of Christianity is tremendously helpful. Such study gives us insight into how we came to be where we are today; where many of our problems came from and, what lessons are to be learned. Having said that however we often make the huge mistake of beginning our reading of history with sometime around the third century AD. The real will and purposes of God are found in the first century of church history. In other words in the context of the New Testament. That is where we meet the people who literally walked and talked with Jesus; the people who sat at His feet and heard His teaching. That is where we meet the apostles to whom the Holy Spirit revealed the foundational truths of our faith. And meditating on those foundational truths allows the Holy Spirit to reveal the wonder of them to our minds and hearts, giving us insight into the will and purpose of God. Then there is a far greater likelihood of us being like the early disciples who lived their lives constantly in the light of the coming again of the Lord Jesus. This in turn spurred them on to creative and effective evangelism. After all, and this is so important for us to keep in mind, the church is *"built on the foundation of the apostles and prophets, Jesus Christ Himself being the corner stone"* (Eph. 2:20).

Remember the Apostle Peter, whose writings provide the core material for this book, wrote to the disciples of his day *"knowing that the laying aside of* [his] *earthly dwelling* [was] *imminent, as the Lord Jesus Christ had made clear to* [him]" (2 Pet. 1:14, see also John 21:18-19). Remember too he wrote as one of the original disciples who *"were eyewitnesses of His majesty"* (2 Pet. 1:16). This Peter was an eye witness of the life and ministry of Jesus. This same Peter was among the first to see Jesus after He rose from among the dead. It goes without saying therefore that we must pay attention to what he has to say as one who is part of the very foundation of the church. He is the one through whom the Holy Spirit says, *"as **each one** has received a special gift, employ it in serving one another as good stewards of the manifold grace of God"* (1 Pet. 4:10). It is therefore patently obvious that there is no way you can effectively use your unique and personal gifting to serve your fellow believers if you are in isolation from them.

There is an important job to be done. Its high time we stopped playing at church. As Peter tells us in verse 7, *"the end of all things is near"*, and he was about to lay down his life for his Saviour and Lord when he said this. Nothing is quite so important while anticipating the imminent return of Christ than that we be *"good stewards of the manifold grace of God"* (v. 10). If we are stewards (caretakers; protectors) of God's grace then we are accountable as to how we fulfill that stewardship. *"We will all stand before the judgement seat of God...So then each of us will give an account of himself to God"* (Rom. 14:10-12; see also 1 Cor. 3:13). Surely it is of paramount importance that we do things in accordance with the will of God as revealed in Scripture.

It is clear from Romans 12:5-13 that gifts are given to effectively operate in the context of the body of Christ. Paul, writing to *"all who are beloved of God in Rome"* (Rom. 1:7), says, *"so we who are many are one body in Christ, and individually members one of another. Since we have gifts that differ according to the grace given to us, each of us is to exercise them accordingly..."*

I love to read the book of Joshua. Imagine being called upon to fill Moses's shoes! Yet, when the time came for Joshua to do exactly that, God gave him some promises which were to be with him for the rest of his life. God's call was to go with the people of Israel and cross the river Jordan, *"to the land which I am giving them"* (Josh. 1:2). Joshua is a shining example of how, as someone else has put it, "God does not call the equipped, He equips the called." They were going to *"the land **which I am giving them**"* but the promise to Joshua was, *"every place on which the soul of your foot treads, **I have given it to you....**"* (v. 3). In other words, as you move forward in obedience to my direction I will give you the land, but one foot print at a time. What a powerful lesson there is here. Remembering that you, as a child of God, are uniquely and individually gifted, there is now no excuse for not being used by God. There is now no place for false humility and lame excuses. Take one step of obedience today in exercising your God given gift and watch what God will do. Nothing will contribute more to your growth in the Lord like one step of obedience.

Joshua could have been forgiven for allowing the thought of filling Moses's shoes to overwhelm him. But God made another wonderful promise, *"as I have been with Moses, I will be with you; I will not fail you or forsake you"* (v. 5). This is exactly the promise God gave me many years ago when my dearest friend, mentor and confidant was taken home to Heaven to be with the Lord. At one time I dreaded the day when he would be taken from me. The very day of his funeral my reading of Scripture "happened" to be in Joshua chapter one. I can't adequately express what that meant to me but I can tell that over the twenty two years since that day God has been totally faithful to that promise.

Several times over, following the promise being given to Joshua, God encouraged him to *"be strong and courageous."* There were times of defeat and discouragement; sometimes because of the weaknesses of others and sometimes because of his own, but ultimately Joshua triumphed because God was ever totally faithful.

I am well aware that when it comes to committing yourself to a local church the knowledge you have of the weaknesses and short comings in that fellowship can be very discouraging and, if allowed, can become a complete "turn off." Back to Joshua for a moment; when the time came to actually begin moving forward, exercising the gifts of leadership which God had given him, Joshua demonstrated he had learned the secret was in taking God at His word. Its a new Joshua who speaks to the people in chapter 3 verse 5, *"Consecrate yourselves, for tomorrow the Lord will do wonders among you."* His eyes are no longer on the good old days of Moses time. His eyes are now on the LORD, Yahweh, the one who revealed Himself to Moses as *"I AM"* (Ex. 3:13-15) and the One who had spoken to him. I'm sorry but I feel many churches are so weak and ineffective because so many of us are focused on all the wrong things; the Pastor who can't walk on water, the elders who, believe it or not, are more human than we thought, or the programs which come and go with monotonous regularity leaving everyone questioning if they are really worth all the effort. Until we have our focus on the living God as revealed to us in Jesus Christ, we will continue to be dissatisfied and the situation will never improve. It all boils down to whether or not we are willing to be men and women who are totally consecrated to the Lord. That means surrendering all rights to myself so that Jesus Christ holds absolute sway over my whole being as my Lord and Master. We are called to be disciples of Christ, not associates. We then become Joshua like and move forward in humble and unquestioning obedience to God's revealed word. In his wonderful devotional book, *My Utmost for His Highest,* Oswald Chambers puts it so powerfully when he says, "Obey God in the thing He shows you, and instantly the next thing is opened up. One reads tomes on the work of the Holy Spirit, when one five minutes of drastic obedience would make things as clear as a sunbeam."[12]

The challenge therefore is; am I willing to take my eyes off the failings and shortcomings of my local church, repent of sin and wrong attitudes in my own heart, surrender totally to Christ as Lord and move forward in obedience no matter what.

The following story illustrates the point. An acquaintance of our's had spent years in a wheelchair. The Lord began stirring in her life and she became convinced God had a ministry for her. As this conviction grew she was made aware that the wheelchair had become her place of security and, in her case, was a hindrance to what God wanted to do in her and through her. It was a great day when she surrendered her whole life to Christ as Lord. This meant He was now her security and her ability for all He might want her to do. The first step from which she never looked back was to get up out of that chair. Many years of effective service followed.

For many of us our security is in our own comfort zone. Many churches are merely existing too; quite content to be in their comfort zone. Good numbers are attending each Sunday, the budget is being met. Whether or not the gospel is being creatively communicated in the surrounding community is another matter.

I've lost count of the number of times, when encouraging people to use their God given gifts for His glory, I've been told, "I have no idea what my gift might be." If that rings bells for you, keep reading.

Challenge

Since there is no doubt you are gifted of God if you truly belong to the body of Christ, the question is, are you willing to move forward and allow the Lord to do exactly what He wants to do in you and through you? In all your difficulties in finding a "suitable church" what really motivates you? Could

---

12   Oswald Chambers; *My Utmost for His Highest*; Barbour Books; October 10th devotional

it be you need to come at the question as to which church you join from a completely different view point? Are you willing to allow the Lord to get you out of your spiritual wheel chair so that you begin to take steps of "drastic obedience." That is the only way you will begin to lose sight of the failings which, at the moment, you see in the local church. You will then be a new person with a new vision, a new joy and a new anointing. Just think about that in prayer for a time.

TEN

I Can Be All God Wants Me to Be

It was a hard lesson for me to learn that being in the will of God was not so much a matter of where I was, but rather who I was in Christ. Following many battles having that realization begin to dawn upon my spirit was like feeling the morning summer sun dispelling the early chill and enveloping me in the warmth and joy of a beautiful new day. Being primarily concerned about who rather than where means sensing the peace and joy of God's nearness as never before. It means knowing that wherever I may be I will never be outside the scope of His presence. All that concerns me now is being available to my Lord and Master. Not only will He make me effective in the now, but He will open the where in His own time. It is oh so freeing. There is absolutely no room for egotism in the matter. As Paul puts it in 1 Corinthians 15:10, *"but by the grace of God I am what I am."*

The word in the New Testament for "gift" is charisma in the original Greek language. It means a gift of grace or as W. E. Vine puts it, "God's endowment on believers by the operation of the Holy Spirit in the churches."[13] It ought to be very clear by this time that everything we have talked about so far, based on 1 Peter 4:7-11, is only possible through the operation of the Holy Spirit. What we are discussing now is no exception. Today's church has adopted the unfortunate attitude of believing that to serve in the local church a person has to be trained first. While training has its place (I thank God for my Bible School experience) we are trained because we already are gifted. We are not trained in order

---

13   W. E. Vine; *Vine's Complete Expository Dictionary of Old and New Testament Words*

to become gifted. Paul's words in 2 Timothy have added significance being among the last of his writings. In chapter 1 verse 6 he says, *"...kindle afresh the gift of God which is in you through the laying on of my hands."* The New International Version says, *"fan into flame the gift of God that is within you."* In other words the gift is already there. God put it there the moment you were reconciled to Him through faith in Christ, that same moment when the Holy Spirit took up residence on the inside of you. At that moment that gift was imparted to you. You became part of Christ Himself. The gift is the product of His resurrection life in you. No one else is gifted quite like you. You are that part of His body through which He is able to uniquely give expression to some aspect of His life and love. How thrilling is that?

As a young Christian I was so blessed in the churches where I was led to the Lord, baptized and nurtured in my walk with God. To this day I can vividly remember the excitement when anticipating attending on Sundays for worship and teaching from God's word, or Tuesdays for prayer and further Bible study with my brothers and sisters in Christ. Those churches seemed to recognize they had a job to do. People were going into eternity without Christ as Saviour. There was therefore an urgency and definite purpose in being part of those churches. As young people we were encouraged to develop our gifts by being given the opportunity to do so under the watchful eye of the leadership. I suppose you could say there was a certain amount of trial and error about this process. But there was also a certain amount of discernment on the part of the older Christians. This was part of the process of both discovering and, having discovered, developing our God given gifting. We were left in no doubt that it was all contributing to a very important cause, seeing people coming to faith in Christ, being baptized and, in turn, becoming active in the local church. You can take it from me, the people in the respective communities were aware of the presence of those churches and what their purpose was. There were individuals gifted in preaching, in music, in administration, in practical helping, in visiting sick people, in caring for families and individuals in need. Some were gifted in the area of strengthening the church body, while others were gifted in reaching out to the community in evangelism.

Before I go any further, it must be said that many churches today are stagnating because they have become too insular. Life flowing into the body through worship, teaching and fellowship must be given an outlet so that it can flow out to lost people in the surrounding community. Jesus words must **never** be forgotten, *"As Moses lifted up the serpent in the wilderness, even so **must** the Son of Man be lifted up"* (John 3:14) (emphasis mine). Your local church exists to lift up Jesus Christ in the community. Each member, as gifted by God, allowing the Lord to work in them and through them is what makes that happen.

You see, there is an important job to be done. As we gather to worship on Sunday we give expression to all the Lord has been showing us about Himself as we have walked with Him throughout another week. Worship is never about us, it is all about Him. He alone is worthy to be worshipped. We hear the word of God preached in the local church and this is designed to build us up in our faith and to equip the saints *"for the work of service, to the building up of the body of Christ"* (Eph. 4:12). That equipping ought to mean we are using our gifts more effectively so that our local church is truly doing its job in the community; people are being brought to faith in the Lord Jesus and the church is growing in the New Testament sense of the word. It is growing, not by people constantly coming in from other churches but because local people are coming to know Christ and, in turn, becoming fruitful members of His body.

Bearing all that in mind, you can see that being used by God according to our individual gifting ought to be a joy and never a drag. Your gifting is part of who you are in Christ. So how do you know what your gifting is, or how can you be sure of what it is? The first question to ask is, are you filled with the Holy Spirit? Since being filled with the Holy Spirit is not an optional extra for the Christian but a command to be obeyed, be sure to be done with all false humility, which gives the impression a person saying they are filled with the Spirit is exhibiting pride. No, the bottom line is if I am not filled with the Spirit I am being disobedient. The command comes in Ephesians 5:17-21; *"So then do not be foolish, but understand what the will of the Lord is. And do not get drunk with wine, for that is dissipation,* **but be filled with the Spirit,** *speaking to one another in Psalms and hymns and spiritual songs, singing and making melody with your heart to the Lord; always giving thanks for all things in the name of our Lord Jesus Christ to God, even the Father; and be subject to one another in the fear of Christ."* In my first book, *So Why Do I Need The Bible?*, I quote A. W. Tozer who helpfully outlines steps to be taken in being filled with the Spirit. Briefly, they are:

1. Be sure you can be - there is no deluxe edition of the Christian life. Being filled with the Spirit is the norm.
2. You must want to be - It means Jesus will be Lord of all in your life
3. Are you sure you need to be? - There must be a deep longing to be filled with the Spirit.

Therefore:

Present your body to the Lord –*"…present your bodies a living and holy sacrifice, acceptable to God, which is your spiritual service of worship. And do not be conformed to this world, but be transformed by the renewing of your mind, so that you may prove what the will of God is, that which is good and acceptable and perfect"* (Rom. 12:1-2).

Ask to be filled –*"So I say to you, ask, and it will be given to you; seek, and you will find; knock, and it will be opened to you…if you then, being evil, know how to give good gifts to your children, how much more will your heavenly Father give the Holy Spirit to those who ask Him"* (Luke 11:9-13).

Be obedient – *"And we are witnesses of these things; and so is the Holy Spirit, whom God has given to those who obey Him"* (Acts 5:32).

Being filled with the Holy Spirit elevates our service in the Lord's name from being a chore which is expected of us to a joyous expression of the life of Christ within us.

The Spirit filled Christian ought never to be thought of as a cut above everyone else. If you are rejoicing in being filled with God's Holy Spirit you will be deeply aware that this is only by God's grace and totally undeserved. Being filled with the Holy Spirit is not something you need to tell people about. They will see it without you saying a word. If for a single moment you or I even begin to think we are somehow superior that is an indication we are not filled with God's Spirit at all. Humbling ourselves in repentance is the only way to deal with such an attitude. On the other hand if, by God's grace, you are rejoicing in being filled with the Spirit then the next step is to seek the Lord as to what your gifting might be. Again, as outlined in my first book, here are some pertinent questions to be asked as suggested by Donald Bridge:

> Do I feel drawn to some particular ministry?
> Am I aware of a need in that ministry?
> Has that ministry a place in my prayers?
> Do responsible Christians encourage me in that ministry?
> When I move forward in that ministry (in cautious faith) do things happen?
> Are my natural talents surrendered to God?

Some years ago I had the great privilege of hearing the late Dr. Paul Brand preaching. He was a missionary doctor and one recognized as a world authority on the disease of leprosy. His message that day had to do with our gifting as Christians. He vividly demonstrated the value and importance of the various organs in our bodies even the ones which, because we can't see them we don't think about them. We don't think about them until something goes wrong with any of them that is. It is then we become aware of how valuable those organs are and that we could not live without them. In the course of his message Dr. Brand said emphatically, "I have a beautiful liver!" His point was powerfully made. We can't see our liver, we are not aware of our liver so long as it is doing its job. But if something goes wrong with it, or it stops functioning, then the entire body ceases to function as it should. His point was also power-fully taken. There are members of the body of Christ who are wonderfully gifted but when they are using their gifts no one is aware of them doing so. They are seldom seen and rarely heard from. But if such people are taken ill, or if the Lord takes them home to Heaven, that is when we all suddenly become aware of what they did and of how much we owe to them.

We must never lose sight of the fact that, as Paul teaches in 1 Corinthians 12, all the gifts are given *"for the common good"* (v. 7). All the gifts given to the church are gifts from the same Holy Spirit; *"but one and the same Spirit works all these things, distributing to each one individually just as He wills"* (v. 11). There is no room whatsoever for complaint or envy, *"but now God has placed the members, each one of them, in the body, just as He desired"* (v. 18). No member can ever be looked upon as super-fluous or less important. It must be remembered that the New Testament picture is that of a healthy body which only functions as each member, seen and unseen, fulfills the role for which it was designed. That is why each of us exercises our gifting to build up and strengthen the others so that they in turn will be effective in the use of their gift. In other words those gifted in administration, giving or practical helps are making it possible for those in public ministry like preaching and teaching to be able to devote themselves to that ministry. Those with public gifts, on the other hand, are building up those with less public gifts. The end result is a healthy body. It is no accident that the two chapters in First Corinthians dealing with gifts, chapters 12 and 14, have "the love chapter sandwiched between them." Chapters 12, 13 and 14 form a complete section. The kind of love that *"does not take into account a wrong suffered"* (1 Cor. 13:5), will constantly and selflessly have the best good of the other members of the body in mind. Such ministry is only interested in giving and not in receiving.

Challenge

The only way you or I as disciples of Jesus will ever bring glory to God while on this earth is by serving Him as He has gifted us. To try to do anything other than this is grieving to the Holy Spirit and brings dishonor on the Lord's name. To be envious of someone else's gift or to try to imitate someone else's gift accomplishes absolutely nothing. It needs to be asked therefore, do you know what your gift from the Lord is? If you don't, what do you plan to do about that? Please pray through the suggestions made in this chapter and if necessary get help from a mature Christian.

ELEVEN

I Must Be Kept Accountable

If who I am in Christ is more important that where I am in His service, then it is equally true that the daily learning curve of life is more important than arriving. It was Oswald Chambers who said, "What we call process, God calls the end...God is not working towards a particular finish; His end is the process... if we realize that obedience is the end, then each moment as it comes is precious."[14] No circumstance in life need ever be wasted for the Christian. No matter how bad things may become, we have a choice. We can choose to surrender to the Lordship of Christ in the particular circumstance, thus allowing Him to teach us what we need to learn or we can complain and rebel and so miss God's best. After all God's best is not what I may imagine it to be. God's best is the reality of His presence and peace and the reproduction of Himself in me and through me. This is the absolutely unique characteristic of the Christian's walk with God as opposed to religious strivings to be something in the distant future. Enjoying God in the moment is the essence of being faithful to the end.

Has it dawned on you yet; it took a long time for it to dawn on me, that when we stand at the judgement seat of Christ, *"each one of us will give an account of himself to God"* (Rom. 14:12). Now the judgement seat of Christ is not about sin being judged. That happened when Jesus died on the cross, *"He, having offered one sacrifice for sins for all time, sat down at the right hand of God, waiting from that time onward until His enemies be made a footstool for His feet. For by one offering He has perfected for all time those who are sanctified"* (Heb. 10:12-14). The judgement seat of Christ is about rewards for faithful service and faithful service is not

---

14   Oswald Chambers; *My Utmost for His Highest*; July 28th

measured in terms of quantity but in terms of quality. The biblical picture in 1 Corinthians 3 is of building on a foundation and that foundation in Jesus Christ, *"for no man can lay a foundation other than the one which is laid, which is Jesus Christ"* (1 Cor. 3:11). The emphasis is on the materials used, *"gold silver, precious stones, wood, hay, straw."* The test is all about the quality of those materials. The testing fires will consume wood, hay and straw but gold, silver and precious stones will endure the test.

In recent years in the part of the world where my wife and I live there has been a major crisis which has come to be known as the "leaky condo crisis." Comparatively new blocks of condominiums have had to undergo extensive and hugely expensive structural repairs because of significant deterioration due to poor quality materials, having been used in the building process. Those condominiums looked wonderful from the outside, but when the real test came what could not be seen was exposed. It was the poor quality of the building materials that was exposed.

Dear reader, can you identify with me when I tell you there have been times in my life when things in my walk with God and in my ministry may have looked good from the outside, but I know and God knows the quality of the materials used was distinctly inferior. I now know the main reason for this was because, at that time, it was my ministry and not His ministry through me. There is an eternity of difference between ministry which is mine and ministry which is His through me. At the judgement seat of Christ there will be no lame excuses and no passing of bucks. The buck will stop with you and the buck will stop with me because, *"each man's work will become evident; for the day will show it because it is to be revealed with fire, **and the fire will test the quality of each man's work.** If any man's work which he has built on it remains, he will receive a reward. If any man's work is burned up, he will suffer loss; but he himself will be saved, yet so as through fire"* (1 Cor. 3:13-15). It ought to be fairly obvious therefore that building with quality materials is a moment by moment exercise. At any particular stage in the building process, when I am exercising my spiritual gift in my own fleshly energy or with wrong motives that is when the materials are inferior. I may cover this up but when I stand before the Lord it will be exposed and burned up. What a moment it was for me when it dawned upon me that a life of quality and faithfulness is made up of moments of quality and faithfulness. Surrendered moments are quality moments because ministry is then His ministry not mine. This is gold, silver and precious stones. This is to be busy yet, at the same time to enjoy rest (Matt. 11:29). This is to bear fruit where you are planted (John 15:5). This is to enjoy *"green pastures and quiet waters"* (Ps. 23:2). This is to make each moment count (Rom. 8:12, 13).

The passage of Scripture upon which this book is based, 1 Peter 4:7-11, begins, you will recall, with the stark statement, *"the end of all things is near, therefore…"* The question needs to be asked again, do you really believe that? Do I really believe that? It is this thought that we may all be with the Lord, provided we know Him as personal Saviour and Lord, sooner than we imagine that ought to grip our attention. Yes, I know Peter's words were written a very long time ago and we are still here. But it is Peter himself who tells us the reason the Lord Jesus has not yet fulfilled His promise to return. *"The Lord is not slow about His promise, as some count slowness, but is patient toward you, not wishing for any to perish but for all to come to repentance. **But the day of the Lord will come like a thief,** in which the heavens will pass away with a roar and the elements will be destroyed with intense heat, and the earth and its works will be burned up"* (2 Pet. 3:9-10). If you read on in this passage you will discover that Peter's challenge is to holiness and godliness in how we live.

So many things in church life would change if we really believed in the temporariness of everything in this life. After all what will happen when we are with the Lord is all that really matters; *"the things which are seen are temporal, but the things which are not seen are eternal"* (2 Cor. 4:18). When I was thinking about this the other day and praying about how to communicate such momentous things, I felt it ought to be done by concentrating on the sheer joy of our relationship with the Lord. After all, we have been reconciled to God; every sin has been forgiven, never to be held against us again (1 John 1:7); all guilt is gone and we have been given a new start (Heb. 9:14). Life now has a quality about it which was impossible before (2 Cor. 5:17). We are no longer living in hope, striving by our own efforts to merit Heaven. We are now *"exult[ing] in hope of the glory of God"* (Rom. 5:2). This changes everything as far as how we view eternity is concerned. Yes, the fact that we will stand before the judgement seat of Christ one day is a solemn thought, but it is only solemn if we have things in our lives which are grieving to the Holy Spirit. It is only solemn if what we are doing is producing results which will be burned up one day when we stand before the Lord. The day Isobel and I were married had a solemn aspect to it; we were making a life long commitment to one another after all. At the same time however there was great joy and rejoicing at the prospect of being together for the rest of our lives. No, we haven't done things right all the time. But being honest with one another, learning to communicate effectively with one another, we have grown in our relationship and in our love for one another. The joy is still there even after forty six years. If we are really walking with the Lord by being in His word and in prayer every day, we will be growing in our relationship with Him. If we are available to tell others our story about what Christ has come to mean in our lives, our joy will know no bounds. If we are using our gifts for the glory of God in the context of our local church which is how He designed them to be used, we will be experiencing the comfort and encouragement that comes from shared life with other members of Christ's body. Then the prospect of being with Christ in eternity becomes something to be anticipated with joy. The prospect of standing before the Lord Jesus at the judgement seat to receive our rewards is no longer a depressing thought but a glorious and thrilling prospect. The prospect of reigning with Him one day is no longer a point of theology to be debated; a matter merely for intellectual exercise. It is now so important that the whole of life here on earth is geared in preparation for it. So, that gift we have received from our risen Lord, we will, *"employ it in serving one another as good stewards of the manifold grace of God"* (1 Pet. 4:10).

Before we go any further, a touchy subject has to be considered. This is important because, as I have discovered through talking with many people over the years, it is the reason why certain people are not actively involved in a local church body. Please take note of the fact that our gifts are to be used *"in serving one another"* (1 Pet. 4:10). People in leadership and shepherding God's people must never be *"lording it over"* them or doing it *"for sordid gain"* (1 Pet. 5:2-3). If you are a control freak, or one given to manipulating others, you have some things you need to sort out before the Lord. Otherwise there will be more wood, hay and straw at the judgement seat than you care to imagine. Biblical leadership is servant leadership. I love the example set by the Lord Jesus in John chapter 13 where we are told about Him getting down on the floor and washing His disciples' feet. Reading the story you will see that He did this, *"knowing that His hour had come,"* (v. 1), and, *"knowing that the Father had given all things into His hands, and that He had come from God and was going back to God,"* (v. 3). In other words Jesus served in the context of the much bigger picture. He was only ever interested in doing the will of His Father, which involved going to the cross and providing eternal salvation for humankind. In other words, everything He did was with eternity in view. I think it was the late Dr. Selwyn Hughes who said about Jesus as portrayed in John 13:1-11, that because He knew why He was here and because He knew He had come from God and was going back to God, "He had nothing to prove." Praise God because Jesus was so secure in who He was, why He was here, and where He was going that He did not ever need to be involved in manipulating anyone or seeking to control anyone for His own ends. He willingly got down on the floor and washed His disciples' feet. When it comes therefore to using our gifts in serving in the body of Christ, **He is our example**. Being a Christian means many things not least of them being that we know who we are (members of Christ's body with His resurrection life on the inside of us). We know why we are here; *"to walk in a manner worthy of the Lord, to please Him in all respects, bearing fruit in every good work and increasing in the knowledge of God"* (Col. 1:10). We also know where we are going, *"to depart and be with Christ, for that is very much better"* (Phil. 1:23).

There is therefore no room whatsoever for either controlling or manipulating one another. Some people know they are manipulators and controllers; others don't seem to know they fit those categories. If you are one who knows this is a problem in your life, I urge you to be willing to humble yourself before the Lord, being willing to repent and seek the Lord that He would root it out of you completely. It could be that some godly counseling would help. If you are reading this and know of someone who does not seem to know they fall into the category of controller or manipulator, then, after a great deal of prayer, go to that person and in a humble spirit talk it over with them. The book of Proverbs tells us that, *"faithful are the wounds of a friend, but deceitful are the kisses of an enemy"* (Prov. 27:6). This is an aspect of being part of a local church which, if adhered to, would help avoid a great deal of heartache and division. Moving on to the judgement seat of Christ is far too real and important an issue to allow a controlling and manipulative spirit, which is usually behind the curse of church politics, to create more and more wood, hay and straw in our lives and in our churches. May the Lord help us to be done forever with hidden agendas. We are called to *"walk in the light as He is in the light,"* and, have you ever noticed the outcome if we do this; *"we have fellowship with one another, and the blood of Jesus Christ His Son cleanses us from all sin"* (1 John 1:7). It is impossible to walk in the light as Christ is in the light and not to have fellowship with one another. Controlling and manipulating one another means we are neither walking in the light, nor do we know anything about having fellowship with one another.

In his autobiography, *Just As I Am,* Dr. Billy Graham tells of the time he was asked if anything surprised him as he looked back over the long years of ministry. "The brevity of it" was the thing that sprang into his mind. Then he made a very interesting statement when he said, "One lesson is to remind us of our responsibility to be diligent in our service for God right now. I may not be able to do everything I once did (nor does God expect me to), but I am called to be faithful to what I can do." This ought to be a challenge and, at the same time an encouragement to all of us no matter how young or old we may be. If you are young I would urge you with all my heart to know how God has gifted you, and make sure you use that gift in your local church. I have already mentioned that the great tragedy in so many people is not being active in a local church, is that so much "gift" is dormant. The body of Christ is greatly impoverished as a result. If you are older; it is never too late. Make a fresh start with God today. Surrender yourself and the years that are left and allow the Holy Spirit to use you to bring enrichment to the people within your local church and beyond. God is able to *"restore the years the locusts have eaten."* At one time in my life great discouragement led to disobedience. As a result I almost missed out on a whole lifetime adventure in the service of the Lord Jesus. I urge you strongly, don't allow anything to stand in the way of being all that God has for you, and all that He wants to do through you. Four decades on and I still thank God constantly that He brought me to deep repentance in my time of discouragement and disobedience. Like Jonah who ran away from the will of God for his life and ended up in despair in the belly of a big fish, *"the word of the Lord came to [me] the second time"* (Jon. 3:1). At one time I honestly thought I was on the scrap heap as far as serving the Lord was concerned. But, praise God, He is the God of the second chance. And, by the way, when I, having heard the word of the Lord for a second time, went to the leadership of my local church, greatly humbled and prepared to make a fresh start, they were so gracious and encouraging. Through my experience they and some others learned some deep lessons which made them more sensitive in handling such matters. Rather than staying away from your local church, how much better it would be were you to lay aside all your grievances; all your own agendas, and humbly submit to the leadership in your church. We all know they are just as human as ourselves. Never forget, it is amazing what God will do with someone with a true feet washing attitude. You can take it from me, nothing is so powerful in breaking down barriers and prejudices. Nothing is more effective in bringing healing to broken relationships. Remember, when Jesus washed the disciples' feet, Judas was among them.

I have some very dear friends in England who are shepherds. A few years ago around lambing season I was privileged to be taken out on to the South Downs near Eastbourne to see first hand all that was going on in one particular flock of sheep. I was amazed at the care and attention given to those animals. It was not a question of what one might call blanket care. I discovered that the shepherd was sometimes out among the sheep almost day and night, especially during the lambing season. The entire future of the flock depended on the quality of care and in many instances, the care was given on an individual basis. The shepherd sometimes came close to exhaustion and I'm sure, were they able to verbalize how they felt, the sheep would say they were forever grateful. One of the main reasons why so many people are so disillusioned with local church life is right here. It is also in this connection that non-believers are often heard to say, "I feel attracted to Jesus Christ but its His followers I can't stand." Shepherding of God's people simply is not happening as it ought to be happening. There is very little sense of what could be called mutual accountability in so many churches. Pastors and elders are called to be under shepherds, see 1 Peter 5:1-5. They are called upon to exercise their ministry in the light of the day when the "Chief Shepherd appears." That is the day when they will receive *the unfading crown of glory,*" one of five crowns mentioned in the New Testament for various aspects of service in the Lord's name. In other words they are accountable to the Lord Jesus, the Chief Shepherd. The sheep, on the other hand, are charged with being accountable to those who are *"over you in the Lord."* Again I emphasize, were such things taken much more seriously by all of us in Christ's body, books like this one would be totally unnecessary.

It is no exaggeration to say there is no body of people on earth which comes close to being so unique as the true body of Christ. Over many years I have had the privilege of ministering in a great variety of healthy local churches. I am constantly reminded that only in the body of Christ and only because each individual has the risen Lord Jesus living on the inside of them by His Holy Spirit, would you find such a unlikely mixture of individuals able to worship together, serve together and love one another with a love which is so much more than outward show. Such a group of people is a joy to be among because they are such a living expression of the very life of the

Lord Jesus. Why don't we see this more than we do? Is it possible to see it more than we do?

I'm pretty certain the readers of this book are people who genuinely want to be part of a local church where the presence and power of God are evident. They want to be part of a church which is growing through people coming to know the Lord on a regular basis; a church that is alive, not with entertainment, but with the felt power of God among His people. With all my heart I believe it is possible if we are all prepared to pay the price in terms of repentance, rooting out everything that is grieving the Holy Spirit among us thus allowing the glory of the Lord to come down. While it is true revival is a sovereign work of God, it is also true that at the heart of revival is the dethroning of what the late Dr. Selwyn Hughes referred to as, "the god called 'I'." The essence of growth in the knowledge of God and of effective, fruitful service in His name is *not I but Christ"* (Gal. 2:20). The answer to the question, *So Why Do I Need A Church?* or, which church do I join, will never be adequately answered until we are prepared to take the god of "self" from the throne of our lives; crowning Jesus absolute Lord and Master so that everything in our lives is worshipfully submitted to His rule. Only then will we be done with what we want or think we need and be concerned only with *"what the will of God is, that which is good and acceptable and perfect"* (Rom. 12:2). May God help us to understand that being active in a local church is not about us. It is all about expressing Christ's life through each member of His body. It is all about Christ having absolute preeminence. It is all about the greater glory of His wonderful name.

Recently I had the great privilege of making an extended visit to the church in Scotland from which Isobel and I were sent out into the ministry of evangelism and Bible teaching over four decades ago. The outstanding memory from the visit is of the Sunday morning worship times when we all met around the Lord's table to remember Him in taking bread and wine as Jesus requested His people to do. I find it so wonderful and amazing that a group of people from a variety of backgrounds and age groups, with such a wide range of personalities, can be so united in worshipping the Lord Jesus. This is the kind of gathering of human beings that only God's grace could put together. In their expression of life as a body of God's people they are all individually gifted and in this area too the variety is remarkable. In 1 Peter 4:10 Peter tells us that when we use our individual gifts we are *"serving one another as good stewards of the manifold grace of God."* The Greek word for "manifold" is *poikilos* (poy-kee-los) which literally means "many colored." In those communion services in Scotland I found it so moving to experience such a high standard of worship. The Lord's people were telling Him all they had come to appreciate about Him. There was a great sense of worshipping, submissive reverence and love. Jesus was being glorified and it was all a beautiful expression of that many colored aspect of God's amazing grace.

There is a very interesting expression of this in Paul's prayer in Ephesians 3:14-21. In it he talks about Christ living in the hearts of those believers by faith. Picture the situation. Here is another "many colored" group of Christians, each one having Christ living on the inside of them. His prayer is *that* they would be, *"rooted and .grounded in love"* with the result that they *"may be able to comprehend **with all the saints** what is the breadth and length and height and depth, and to know the love of Christ which surpasses knowledge, that you may be **filled up to all the fulness of God.**"* Do you see the significance of this great truth? It is impossible to appreciate the love of God in isolation. Only in the fellowship of the body in a local church with each member functioning as gifted by the Lord, can we even begin to appreciate what the love of God means. His love and grace are so "many colored" that they can only be expressed as all the members of His body function in all the variety of their gifting while, at the same time, demonstrating the oneness of the common life they all share. John 1:16 comes to mind; *"of His fulness we have all received, and grace upon grace."*

Challenge

I don't know about you, but for me the whole idea that I am moving on to eternity when I will stand before the Lord is deeply challenging. If Christ really lives in me thus making me part of His body and if He has made me to be part of the expression of His "many colored" grace, I can't begin to contemplate doing this in isolation. Such a thing simply makes no sense whatsoever. I urge you to give that serious thought.

SECTION 4

I Need A Church
Because I need to be highly motivated
1 Peter 4:11

Something to think about...

In this section we are going to be looking at the three things which are at the very heart of the issue being dealt with in this book:

1. The need for anointed preaching of God's word.
2. Service is worthless unless it is done in the energy of the Holy Spirit.
3. The sole objective ought to be the greater glory of God alone.

Any local church which is strong in these three areas will experience the blessing of God and will grow. But for that to happen there will have to be a great deal of heart searching on the part of those currently active in local churches and on the part of those desiring to be.

Joshua 3:5 says, *"Then Joshua said to the people, consecrate yourselves, for tomorrow **the Lord will do wonders among you.**"* Commenting on this verse the great preacher on revival, Leonard Ravenhill said, "Today God is bypassing men - not because they are too ignorant, but because they are too self-sufficient. Our abilities have become our handicaps, and our talents our stumbling blocks."

May the Lord grant us all grace to humble ourselves in His presence and to seek Him for renewal and revival in our churches, so that a new God consciousness will be created in the communities where God has placed us.

TWELVE

Hearing From God is Essential

Do you ever wish you had been there, the day the church was born. It was even more momentous than the time the glory of the Lord came down and filled the Tabernacle in the desert (see Ex. 40:34). So awesome was that moment that Moses was not able to enter the Tabernacle. But when the church was born the glory of God did not come to fill a Tabernacle, Temple or any such thing. The glory of God came upon a group of Christ's humble disciples and, *"they were all filled with the Holy Spirit"* (Acts 2:4). Everything within me leaps for joy when I think of what that must have been like and then I remember that God's word tells me, *"...do you not know that your body is a temple of the Holy Spirit who is in you, whom you have from God, and that you are not your own?"* (1 Cor. 6:19). Think of what that means. At this moment you and I, as believers in the Lord Jesus, have Almighty God dwelling on the inside of us. We are His temple. I'm not sure what that thought does for you, but I find it totally humbling just to think that Almighty God would want to have anything to do with me, quite apart from actually taking up residence within me. Yet, that is exactly what it means.

Why, oh why therefore are our churches not places which are vibrant with the glory of the Lord? Allow me to take you back to the Macedonian Christians mentioned in an earlier chapter. *"They first gave themselves to the Lord"* (2 Cor 8:5). The glory of God will never be real among us until we get this right. This is where being highly motivated begins. This is the difference between commitment and surrender. As pointed out somewhere else, it is possible to be committed without being surrendered. It is possible to be committed and keep something back; like Ananias and his wife Sapphira in Acts 5. They sold a piece of property then, giving everyone the impression they had given all the money gained to the Lord, *"they kept back some of the price."* Even in the atmosphere of all that was happening shortly after the birth of the church their personal greed robbed them of everything. They were unwilling to allow their commitment, which was very real, to go as far as surrender. Had it been surrender they would have kept nothing back. The difference between the Macedonian Christians and Ananias and his wife was that the Macedonians' giving began with the surrender of themselves to the Lord. When I am surrendered, so is everything else. There is no one more highly motivated than the individual who is completely surrendered to Christ as Lord.

It may be helpful at this point to clarify what is meant by being surrendered to Christ as Lord. First of all we are not talking about irresponsible religious fanaticism; the kind which is always quoting scripture, mostly out of context, to justify having things one's own way. Surrender to Christ as Lord involves the entire being. Jesus Himself said in Matthew 22:37-38, *"You shall love the Lord your God with all your heart, and with all your soul, and with all your mind. This is the great and foremost commandment."* Total surrender to Christ is not some mindless exercise therefore. Rather, the complete person is permeated with the love of God and with love for God. The surrendered Christian is not, to borrow a phrase from the late Dr. John Stott, "Keen but Clueless."[15] Surrender to Christ as Lord is also a matter of *"present*[ing] *your bodies a living and holy sacrifice, acceptable to God, which is your spiritual service of worship. And do not be conformed to this world, but be transformed by the renewing of your mind, so that you may prove what the will of God is, that which is good and acceptable and perfect"* (Rom. 12:1-2). Such an act of surrender results in a transformed life because the mind has been renewed. Everything is seen through different eyes. Such a person now has, what has been called, "a Christian world view." There is however another aspect to being surrendered to Christ as Lord and that is my will has to be given over to Him. The

---

15   John R. W. Stott; *Your Mind Matters*; IVP, 1972; Page 9

primary example of the surrendered will is that of the Lord Jesus in the garden of Gethsemane. As He prays to His Father in Luke 22:42 he prays, *"Father if you are willing, remove this cup from me; yet not my will, but Yours be done."* Jesus, knowing all the going to the cross to die for the sin of the world would involve, surrendered Himself completely to the will of His Father in carrying out God's great plan of salvation for the human race. Therefore the challenge to the disciple of Christ is the challenge of the surrendered will. Listen again to the words of the Lord Jesus Himself, *"If anyone wishes to come after Me, he must deny himself, and take up his cross and follow Me"* (Mark 8:34). The crux of everything for the disciple of Christ is, as Paul summed it up in Galatians 2:20, *"not I but Christ...."*

In the local church this principle does not only apply to people in leadership but to each and every member of Christ's body. Every member functioning as gifted by God is what maintains the local church in health and growth. Here in 1 Peter 4:11 however, Peter singles out one particular area of gifting; that of *"whoever speaks."* Such a person has the enormous responsibility of speaking, *"as one who is speaking the utterances of God."* I do not think it is an exaggeration to say that it is in this area of church life, more than any other, where the problem of so many people opting out of church life lies. People opt out because they have tried so many places of worship where the word of God is not being taught as it ought to be. Others who have not yet opted out are going through the church hopping stage. The complaints vary. Sometimes the preaching or teaching is seen as all head and no heart, other times it is all heart and no head. For still others, "the gospel" is not preached regularly enough. Some say that the people are left hanging in the air not knowing what they are supposed to do with what they are hearing. And so it goes on. Dr. Ravi Zacharias hit the nail on the head when he said, "we must reclaim the pulpit."

It is obvious that, in the context of our text, the word "speaks" is referring to authoritative preaching of God's word; the one speaking is to *"do so as one who is speaking the utterances of God."* This is an awesome responsibility indeed. Yes, it is important that we meet in our local churches to worship and to enjoy fellowship with one another. But it is not an exaggeration to say that nothing is more important than authoritative, God anointed preaching and teaching of God's word. This above all else is what contributes to the growth of the body and to the building up of God's people. There is a hunger for God's word out there. Even people who are not yet disciples of Christ want the church to stop waffling about what the Bible says and start to tell it like it is. After all God's word is *"living and active and sharper than any two edged sword, and piercing as far as the division of soul and spirit, of both joints and marrow, and able to judge the thoughts and intentions of the heart"* (Heb. 4:12). Several times over the years I have had the experience of people coming to me in anger following the preaching of God's word, wanting to know who told me all about them. Of course no one had; the Holy Spirit was using God's word to convict them of their sin and need of Christ. It has also happened that a person who was a known satanist fled from a preaching service when the sermon was on Hebrews 2:14, *"…that through death He* [Christ] *might render powerless him who had the power of death, that is the devil, and might free those who through fear of death were subject to slavery all their lives."* The word of God not only has to be preached but preached under the anointing of the Holy Spirit. Then it will do its own work of challenging and changing human hearts.

Before we leave the topic of authoritative, anointed preaching, I must point out a biblical principle, which if not adhered to will mean more and more shallow preaching which does nothing more than tickle the ears of people who *"will not endure sound doctrine, but wanting to have their ears tickled, they will accumulate for themselves teachers in accordance to their own desires"* (2 Tim. 3:3). May I remind you that some of Paul's strongest words on preaching were written in the last of his New Testament letters, 2 Timothy. You don't need me to tell you that people's final words to us are words we usually remember vividly and those words are usually words of urgency. Today's church simply has to "reclaim the pulpit" for authoritative, Holy Spirit anointed preaching and teaching. Nothing else will produce conviction of sin in the hearts of people who do not yet know Christ. Nothing else will challenge the people of God to live lives of holiness. Only this will rescue churches from the current slide into irrelevance in their respective communities. The biblical principle which every preacher who would preach God's word ought to have before their eyes every day is the one given us in 2 Timothy 2:15, *"Be diligent to present yourself approved to God as a workman who does not need to be ashamed, accurately handling the word of truth."* The importance of this verse is seen when it is broken down into its various parts:

The preacher's discipline—diligence, Greek, *spoudazo* (spoo-dad-zo), fully applying oneself with endeavor. His priorities are never in doubt and his time is precious.

The preacher's character—the approval of men is unimportant; God's approval is everything. The Greek word is *dokimos* (dok-ee-mos), confirmed genuine through having God's approval. What does God's approval look like? In 1 Thessalonians 2:4 Paul speaks about being *"approved by God to be entrusted with the gospel, so we speak, not as pleasing men, but God Who examines our hearts."* In other words God's approval was evident because they had endured the testing God had taken them through. James 1:12 says, *"blessed is the man who perseveres under trial; for once he has been approved, he will receive the crown of life which the Lord has promised to those who love Him."* It is very interesting to observe that, almost without exception, the preacher of God's word who is truly anointed by the Holy Spirit in ministry, is one whom God has taken through deep testing. There is a deep godly quality that comes through in the ministry.

The preacher's attitude—"a workman." The Greek word is *ergates* (er-gat-ace), a field laborer. What this meant for Paul is evident in scriptures like 2 Corinthians 6 which makes this point very powerful. In the context of *"working together with Him"*, Paul makes it clear that there is no room for self or selfish ambition in the service of the Lord.

> *"...giving no offense in anything, so that the ministry will not be discredited, but in everything commending ourselves as servants of God, in much endurance, in afflictions, in hardships, in distresses, in beatings, in*

imprisonments, in tumults, in labours, in sleeplessness, in hunger, in purity, in knowledge, in patience, in kindness, in the Holy Spirit, in genuine love, in the word of truth, in the power of God; by the weapons of righteousness for the right hand and the left, by glory and dishonor, by evil report and good report; regarded as deceivers and yet true; as unknown yet well known, as dying yet behold we live; as punished yet not put to death, as sorrowful yet always rejoicing, as poor yet making many rich, as having nothing yet possessing all things."

Do you get the picture? By comparison, preachers in our western society having absolutely nothing to complain about. However we need to keep in mind that many faithful servants of the Lord in other parts of the world are paying a tremendous cost for being faithful to the Lord and to His word.

The preacher's motive — *"...does not need to be ashamed."* The Greek word for ashamed is *anepaischuntos* (an-ep-ah-ee-skhoontos). It is "an intensive adjective" meaning "having no cause for shame"[16]. I have had occasion in the past when, for a time, I have been able to hide from everyone things about which I was ashamed. There are three things about such times I will never forget: a) I could never hide them from myself, b) more importantly, I could never hide them from the Lord and c) they eventually affected the quality of my ministry. There is no preacher on this planet more grateful for the convicting ministry of the Holy Spirit and for the cleansing power in the blood of Christ than the author of this book. With all my heart I would say to my fellow preachers, be constantly humbling yourself before the Lord and deal with things you would be ashamed of whenever the Holy Spirit makes you aware of them. To elders of churches I would say earnestly, if you are sensing something is having an adverse effect on the quality of the speaker's teaching or preaching, in a spirit of love and grace help him pinpoint the problem and deal with it before the Lord. Every time I stand before a congregation to preach or teach God's word I ought to

---

16   W. E. Vine; *Vine's Complete Expository Dictionary of Old and New Testament Words*

do so knowing I am standing before God. Were I to be ushered into God's presence at that moment, would I be ashamed? As I think of this now I'm reminded of a dear friend of many years ago, the late Campbell Reid, who collapsed and died while preaching God's word. Knowing Campbell as I did; his passion for God, his diligence in ministry, I know he would have a joyful entrance into the presence of his Lord and Saviour.

The preacher's image — *"accurately handling the word of truth."* The Greek word here is *orthotomeo* (or-thot-om-eh-o); I cut straight. "In this context...the main idea seems to be that Timothy must be scrupulously straightforward in dealing with *"the word of truth,"* in strong contrast to the crooked methods of the false teachers."[17] The idea that any preacher or teacher of the word of God be remotely concerned about his public image is truly reprehensible. His one and only concern ought to be faithfulness to the text and context of whatever passage of God's word he is teaching or preaching from and to apply that truth in the power of the Holy Spirit. Yes, it is important to be himself, filled with the Holy Spirit. Yes, it is important that he speak clearly and pay attention to proper diction etc. But if before a congregation he is anything other than who he is when alone or at home with his wife and children, then he is wasting everyone's time.

Lots of people can speak but not all of them, by any means, are gifted in the sense of 1 Peter 4:11. The context of Peter's word "speaks" is, *"as each one has received a special gift, employ it in serving one another as good stewards of the manifold grace of God."* It is true, a natural talent for public speaking can be sanctified by the Holy Spirit when the individual is totally surrendered to the Lordship of Christ and filled with the Holy Spirit. But a talent for public speaking must never be confused with a gift to preach or teach God's word. Public speaking and preaching are two very different things. Some sermons which are meant to pass for preaching are nothing more than an exercise in public speaking. What makes preaching recognizable as true preaching is the anointing of the Holy Spirit, which, when present is

---

17   Donald Guthrie, B.D., M.Th; *The Pastoral Epistles,* The Tyndale Press, page 148

felt by the congregation. Such preaching touches the mind on its way to the heart and it moves the will to action. The congregation are left in no doubt as to what they ought to do having heard from God through the preacher. The true preacher never loses sight of the fact that he is meant to be *"a good steward."* In other words his gift is to be held in trust for the whole church.

One of the board members of the ministry I have the privilege of representing, Mr. Al Kelly, once worked as a Crusade Director with The Billy Graham Evangelistic Association. He tells how every time Dr. Graham stood to preach a hush would descend upon the vast crowd. Why did people respond in their hundreds each night? It was because God's word was being preached by a truly gifted preaching evangelist who was also anointed with the Holy Spirit.

Having had the privilege of being touched by the preaching of Billy Graham and the teaching of the late Alan Stibbs and John Stott all I can say is there was a sense of eternity when those men handled the word of God. All of us who have the sacred calling upon our lives to preach and teach God's word ought to be constantly on our faces in God's presence seeking that anointing.

The importance of all this is further emphasized through Peter's words, *"...do so as one speaking the utterances of God."* It is one thing to gather a great deal of material together when preparing sermons, but it is another thing all together to know what word God wants to be delivered. We preachers ought to tremble at the very idea of standing before a congregation without being sure of having the Lord's word for that group of people. In the list of gifts given in Romans chapter six, prophecy is mentioned. It is generally agreed that prophecy in the New Testament means forth telling and not foretelling as in Micah 5:2 for example where the very place of the birth of Christ is foretold. "In such passages as 1 Corinthians 12:28 and Ephesians 2:20, the prophets are placed after Apostles since not the prophets of Israel are intended, but the gifts of the ascended Lord. See also Ephesians 4:8, 11 and Acts 13:1. The purpose of their ministry was to edify, to comfort and to encourage the believers, 1 Corinthians 14:3, 24-25."[18] It is also worth noting that when Paul speaks in Ephesians 2:20 of the church as *"God's household"* being *"built of the foundation of the apostles and prophets, Christ Jesus Himself being the chief corner stone"*, there is only one foundation. That is why we are not talking about prophecy in the sense of that given by the prophets of Israel. As Paul says in 1 Corinthians 3:11, *"for no man can lay a foundation other than the one which is laid, which is Jesus Christ."*

Were there ever more telling words in connection with anointed preaching and teaching, the only kind which will build up the body of Christ, than Paul's in 1 Corinthians 2:4-5. He says there *"my message and my preaching were not in persuasive words of wisdom, but in demonstration of the Spirit and of power, so that your faith would not rest on the wisdom of men, but on the power of God."* It is little wonder Paul's words in 2 Timothy 4:1 (his final letter) are full of such urgency, *"I solemnly charge you in the presence of God and of Christ Jesus, who is to judge the living and the dead, and by His appearing and His kingdom: preach the word; be ready in season and out of season; reprove, rebuke, exhort, with great patience and instruction."* In a "Third Way" interview the late Dr. John Stott made the following comment which every preacher and teacher would do well to take to heart. He said, "The church is always a reflection of the preaching it receives, and I don't think it is an exaggeration to say that the low standards of Christian living throughout the world are due more than anything else to the low standards of Christian preaching and teaching."[19]

Verses 19 and 20 of Psalm 107 are both interesting and powerful: *"Then they cried out to the Lord in their trouble; He saved them out of their distresses. He sent His word and healed them and delivered them from their destructions (or pits)."* You may be one of many people who attend a church these days and, for you, life is "the pits." You enter the building longing to hear a word from the Lord and you come away feeling as bad as ever. You may feel like joining the growing army of people who have stopped attending church for the very same reason. This

---

18   W. E. Vine; *Vine's Complete Expository Dictionary of Old and New Testament Words*

19   Dr. John Stott; *Idea magazine,* September/October 2011, page 38

is a tragedy because, for you, there is no healing word that will help lift you up out of your distresses and destructions. Just thinking about this literally drives me to my knees crying out to God that He will keep me out of pulpits and off platforms if I am not able to stand there having come from the very presence of the Lord with His healing word for the people. What a responsibility. What a privilege.

The late Dr. D. Martyn Lloyd Jones, one of the greatest preachers of the 20th century, tells the following story. He, together with a Pastor and a Doctor visited a young lady who had been paralyzed in both legs for eight years. She had some movement in her legs but was unable to walk. She had been diagnosed as having a form of hysteria and it turned out to be so. Her situation was the result of deep disappointment in her emotional life. Her older sister had been coming to church and through sitting under Dr. Lloyd Jones's preaching had come to know the Lord as her personal Saviour. After some time a second sister came to church and was saved through the preaching of God's word. Eventually both the sisters who had found the Lord carried the paralyzed one to church. After listening to the word of God for several weeks she too surrendered her life to Christ. No counsellor or pastor spoke with her. She only listened to the anointed preaching of the word of God. Inner healing took place and eventually the paralyses disappeared completely.

Before preaching on one occasion, Dr. Lloyd-Jones said to his congregation, "I am about to say things which are the most wonderful things a human being can ever utter. I am about to tell you some of the most marvellous and mysterious things that a human being can ever hear."[20]

It is said of Dietrich Bonhoeffer that he, "took preaching seriously. For him a sermon was nothing less than the very word of God, a place where God would speak to His people... preaching was not merely an intellectual exercise. Like prayer or meditation on a scriptural text, it was an opportunity to hear from heaven, and for the preacher, it was a holy privilege to be

20   D. Martyn Lloyd-Jones; *Preaching and Preachers*; Hodder and Stoughton

the vessel through whom God would speak. Like the incarnation, it was a place of revelation, where Christ came into this world from outside it."[21]

Describing what it was like to listen to Bonhoeffer preaching one listener observed, "there was something compelling about him when he was preaching. When you saw him preaching...you saw a young man who was entirely in God's grasp."[22]

Dr. Alexander Whyte (1836-1921), a man born out of wedlock and into great poverty was raised up by God to be a powerful preacher of God's word in Scotland. He had enormous influence on students of his day and, indeed, he was so used by God that his influence reached around the world. Allow me to quote extensively about his preaching and pastoral ministry:

> "Above everything else, Whyte was a preacher. Preaching to him meant work. 'I would have all lazy students drummed out of the college', he said, 'and all lazy ministers out of the Assembly. I would have laziness held to be the one unpardonable sin in all our students and in all our ministers.' A voracious reader and a diligent student, Whyte did not neglect his pastoral ministry or his family. In 1898 when Whyte was called to be moderator of the Assembly, he exhorted the pastors to concentrate on humility, prayer and work. 'We have plenty of time for all our work did we husband our time and hoard it up aright,' he told them. 'We cannot look seriously in one another's faces and say it is want of time. It is want of intention. It is want of determination. It is want of method. It is want of motive. It is want of conscience. It is want of heart. It is want of anything and everything but time.' The sales manager of a successful Christian publishing house tells me that pastors are not buying books. 'Most of the books sold in Christian book stores are sold to and read by

---

21   Eric Metaxas; *Bonhoeffer: Pastor, Martyr, Prophet, Spy*; Thomas Nelson; page 272
22   Eric Metaxas; *Bonhoeffer: Pastor, Martyr, Prophet, Spy*; Thomas Nelson; page 277

women', he said. If our pastors are not using their valuable time for study, what are they using it for? Perhaps Whyte had the answer: 'We shroud our indolence under the pretext of a difficulty. The truth is, it is lack of real love for our work."[23]

There is so much to be learned from the great preachers of the past. Those of us who have the immense responsibility and privilege of preaching the word of God would do well to discipline ourselves to read more of their biographies and cry to God that we might learn from their example.

Challenge

Bearing in mind what you have just read may I urge you to spend much more time interceding in God's presence on behalf of preachers and teachers of God's word. Tell those known to you that you are doing this and ask them for specific pointers for you to use in intercession.

Preachers and teachers; let us search our hearts in God's presence about the depth and quality of the spiritual food we are serving the people.

---

23   Warren Wiersbe; *Walking With The Giants: A Minister's Guide to Good Reading and Great Preaching*, Baker Book House; Page 91

THIRTEEN

Knowing God is Paramount

Something is fundamentally wrong. The church in the West claims so much yet appears so sick. Ordinary people look on and see very little to attract them, even less that will convict them, about having a need of God in their lives or about having no hope for eternity. You may be disillusioned with the church because, on the one hand, part of you wants to be part of a church but on the other hand the more you look the more you feel today's church is somehow dysfunctional. This is the very antithesis of how things ought to be where there is Holy Spirit anointed preaching and teaching of God's word. A few moments spent thinking about what it would be like belonging to a church envisioned by Peter in 1 Peter 4:7-11 brings home the realization we are missing something somewhere. The section of verse 11 we are considering now talks about *"serving by the strength which God supplies."* This does not describe how serving is done in today's church. Most of what happens today happens with very little reliance on God. Today we bring in consultants and manuals about programs which seem to work in other places. Today's church has very little idea of the enormity of the spiritual battle we are fighting. Very little is understood about the New Testament expectation that we *"resist the devil and he will flee from you"* (Jas. 4:7). Very little is known about the practice, power and effectiveness of *"intercessions... for all men"* (1 Tim. 2:1).

The question has to be asked; if we are going to serve *"by the strength which God supplies,"* we must be men and women who know what this means experientially. To experience God supplying us with His strength has to stem from knowing Him in a growing, intimate relationship. There is no doubt that the

145

New Testament view of how this works is not one of us working with God tagging along to help. First of all, it is rather us *"working together with Him"* (2 Cor. 6:1), and that may not necessarily mean everything being plain sailing, constantly enjoying the kind of blessing we would like to see. Basically it means, in the context of 2 Corinthians 6, *"giving no cause for offense in anything, so that the ministry will not be discredited, but in everything commending ourselves as servants of God, in much endurance, in afflictions, in hardships, in distresses..."* (2 Cor. 6:3-4). We live in an increasingly hostile world. Are we prepared for that?

The other aspect of experiencing His strength is to have the glorious truth dawn upon us that being a Christian means that Christ literally lives on the inside of us by His Holy Spirit. This gives a new dimension to knowing God and His strength. It is now a question of God working through us because He resides within us. Remember Paul's word in Galatians 2:20, *"it is no longer I who live, but Christ lives in me..."* I know this has been mentioned several times before and I make no apology for mentioning it again because it is right at the heart of everything it means to be a Christian. As a preacher I'm constantly reiterating in God's presence the wonderful words of Jesus in John 15:5, *"...apart from Me you can do nothing."* In fact it is no exaggeration to say that I cannot live a single moment as a Christian for the glory of God apart from Him.

Difficult as it is to say, I think serious questions have to be asked as to what "gospel" is being preached in our churches. It is very sadly possible to have many people in churches who enjoy being there and everything is designed to make them feel comfortable but, if the truth be known, they know nothing of Christ living in them and working through them.

Speaking as an evangelist I have to say that while it is an enormous privilege and joy to preach the gospel; no other message can tell us where we came from, why we are here and where we are going. But very rarely, and I search my own heart here regarding my own preaching, are people confronted with why they need Christ in the first place. Very rarely are people challenged about repenting of sin and making a personal commitment to Christ as Saviour and Lord. People don't know how to respond to the gospel. They are rarely challenged about living holy lives having made that response. All this begs the question, what "gospel" ought we to be preaching? It is an enormous responsibility to preach the gospel. Preaching it is never to be taken lightly. In fact, the more aware I am of the content and implications of the real gospel, the more aware I will be that it ought never to be preached without first a great deal of time having been spent in prayer. It will be a shallow gospel that is preached without a deep awareness of our true condition, if we don't know Christ and of the dire consequences of rejecting Him. The faithful preacher of the gospel will have shed many tears over the lostness of people who don't know Christ. He will be deeply aware of the fact that only the Holy Spirit can convict people of how sinful sin is, and how awful eternity will be if they are never reconciled to God. That is why the gospel is good news. It is so much more that simply having a ticket to Heaven and then continuing to live like everyone else. The point of the whole exercise is that we desperately need to be reconciled to our creator God and, until that happens, we are totally without hope for eternity. The very worst thing we preachers can do is water this message down in an effort to make it more palatable and, what is nearer the truth, to avoid becoming unpopular. Allow me to simply and briefly outline the main points of the Gospel:

Human kind was created by Almighty God on the sixth day of creation. We are not animals. We were created in the image of God (Gen. 1:26; 2:7). We possess a moral likeness to our creator and are morally responsible to Him. We each have a conscience and the freedom to make moral decisions. God did not create robots.

Having been tempted by Satan to question God and to consider living independently of God, man made the wrong moral choice. Today he makes excuses; people are angry because they don't have jobs etc., etc. No, man is still making the same wrong moral choice and has no one to blame but himself for the consequences of that choice. The consequences are to have his relationship with his creator broken, to be banished from the presence of his creator and to reap the fruits of listening to the lies of the devil of whom Jesus said, *"in him there is no truth"* and *"he is a liar and the father of lies"* (John 8:44). See also Genesis 3.

Sin has now entered the experience of humanity. Mankind's nature has become corrupted by it. Those of us who are parents and grandparents ought to need no convincing of this. We never have to teach our children and grandchildren how to sin. They, like us before them, find it easier to sin than not. The downward spiral has continued until here we are, living in the last days of this world's history.

Sin has inevitable consequences in the experience of rebellious mankind. In Romans 5:12 we are told, *"Therefore, just as through one man sin entered into the world, and death through sin, and so death spread to all men, because all sinned."* It is not rocket science therefore to see why the same Apostle Paul in another of his letters describes the plight of mankind as being, *"...dead in your trespasses and sins...according to the course of this world, according to the prince of the power of the air, the spirit that is now working in the sons of disobedience. Among them we too all formerly lived in the lusts of our flesh, indulging the desires of the flesh and of the mind, and were by nature children of wrath, even as the rest"* (Eph. 2:1-3). This is why people say things like, "there is no God" or, "I don't know whether there is a God or not."

Almighty God has taken the initiative and in these, the last days of this world's history, He has intervened by making Himself known in the person of His Son, Jesus Christ. As Hebrews 1:1-3 says, *"God, after He spoke long ago to the fathers in the prophets in many portions and in many ways, **in these last days has spoken to us in His Son,** Whom He appointed heir of all things, through Whom also He made the world. And He is the radiance of His glory and the exact representation of His nature, and upholds all things by the word of His power. When He had made purification for sins, He sat down at the right hand of the Majesty on high."* Again, the Bible accurately describes for us what those **last days** would look like. In 2 Timothy 3:1-5 those days are described as days when, *"difficult times will come. For men will be lovers of self, lovers of money, boastful,* *arrogant, revilers, disobedient to parents, ungrateful, unholy, unloving, irreconcilable, malicious gossips, without self-control, brutal, haters of good, treacherous, reckless, conceited, lovers of pleasure rather than lovers of God, holding to a form of godliness, although they have denied its power..."* This is an accurate description of 21st century people. The questions about the existence of God cannot be answered fully without taking into account God's act of intervention. I love the words of Paul immediately following those from Ephesians 2 quoted above, *"**But God** Who is rich in mercy, because of His great love with which He loved us, **even when we were dead in our trans-gressions, made us alive together with Christ** (by grace you have been saved), and raised us up with Him, and seated us with Him in the heavenly places in Christ Jesus..."* (Eph. 2:4-6).

The whole point of God's initiative is that His Son, Jesus Christ, as man's substitute, would deal with man's sin and his resulting separation from God. This is why the gospel is such good news. It is painfully obvious that all man's efforts to improve his condition are woefully inadequate. Whatever anyone says, the worldwide downward spiral as a result of man's sinful condition continues. The amazing and historical facts are that when God in love intervened His whole purpose was to reconcile mankind to Himself. *"God was in Christ reconciling the world to Himself, not counting their trespasses against them..."* (2 Cor. 5:19). Make no mistake, these are among the most momentous words you will ever read. What they are saying is that the Almighty creator against whom mankind has sinned has made Himself known with the sole purpose in mind of reconciling rebellious mankind to Himself. When Jesus died on the cross, He died the death we deserve to die. He took the judgement of God upon Himself in our place. Although it is all totally undeserved, we can now be completely forgiven, our guilt can now be completely removed, we can be reconciled to our creator and live in oneness with Him, filled with new life now and filled with hope for eternity.

Forgiveness now and hope for eternity cannot be earned, only received. God's word could not be clearer on this issue; *"for by grace you have been saved through faith, **and that not of yourselves, it is the gift of God;** not as a result of works so that no* *one may boast"* (Eph. 2:8-9). *"For the wages of sin is death, **but the free gift of God is eternal life in Jesus Christ our Lord"*** (Rom. 6:23). Very clearly this means no amount of good deeds, no amount of religious observance, no amount of self effort will ever merit a place in heaven. There is only one way and that is through accepting God's provision in His Son Jesus Christ. If that offends in any way it is because the one offended is not coming to terms with their true condition in the light of God's perfect holiness. Paul teaches, in Romans 7:13 that God's holy law, the ten commandments, if honestly considered powerfully reveal to me that I am not nearly so good as I thought I was and I'm certainly nothing like as good as I ought to be, if I'm going to be in Heaven by my own good living.

Receiving God's gift is not something ever to be taken lightly. The New Testament lays heavy emphasis on repentance. Repentance literally means a change of mind resulting in a change in direction. One of the best examples of this is in the experience of the Thessalonian Christians. When they came to faith in Christ they, *"turned to God from idols to serve the living and true God and to wait for His Son from heaven, Whom He raised from the dead, that is Jesus, Who rescues us from the wrath to come"* (1 Thess. 1:9-10). In other words they turned away from their lifestyle of worshipping dead idols, and it is not difficult to imagine what that would involve, and they turned their lives over to the living God, realizing that their only hope was in God's Son, Jesus Christ. He now meant everything to them and the focus of their lives was to live in anticipation of His return when they would, *"meet the Lord in the air and so [they would] always be with the Lord"* (1 Thess. 4:13-18). Obviously Jesus had come to mean everything to them. When an individual is filled with the kind of hope only Christ can give, that individual is deeply aware that they owe everything to Him, and that they have nothing apart from Him. It was Oswald Chambers who said, "repentance does not bring a sense of sin, but a sense of unutterable unworthiness. When I repent, I realize that I am utterly helpless."[24] Any person truly born again and enjoying

---

24   Oswald Chambers; *My Utmost for His Highest,* August 22nd

new life in Christ will tell you that it is the very last thing they deserve. They are utterly unworthy of God's gift of eternal life; they receive it by simple faith and with profound gratitude.

There are terrible consequences for rejecting God's provision in Christ. All kinds of intellectual gymnastics are being performed these days to avoid the terrible stark reality of Hell. If Hell, eternal punishment suffered with *"the devil and his angels"* (Matt. 25:41), is not real then Christ's coming into the world, His terrible suffering on the cross at Calvary and His historical resurrection from the dead are all meaningless. The whole point of what He did was to take the judgement of God for sin upon Himself so that humanity could be delivered from the terrible eternal consequences of choosing to live in rebellion against God, rejecting the creator's provision of reconciliation with Himself through Christ. Again the word of God could not be clearer, *"...but now once at the consummation of the ages He has been manifested to put away sin by the sacrifice of Himself. And inasmuch as it is appointed for men to die once and after this comes judgement, so Christ also, having been offered once to bear the sins of many, will appear a second time for salvation without reference to sin, to those who eagerly await Him"* (Heb. 9:27-28).

Yes, knowing God in Christ as outlined above is indeed paramount. May I encourage you to examine your heart as you read this book to make sure this is the kind of relationship you have with your creator, having been reconciled to Him through Jesus Christ. Whatever church you become part of will always only be a pleasant appendage on your life until you see the full significance of what it means to be reconciled to God. Because it means Jesus Christ is absolute Lord of every part of your life; family, career, time, money, possessions, church life, all is geared towards where and how you can be most effective in serving the Lord and His people. I trust it is becoming clear now that that is in your local church. The only way such service can possibly be performed effectively is service which is *"by the strength which God supplies"* (1 Pet. 4:11). Just thinking about that fills me with a profound sense of gratitude to the Lord. Everything is transformed when we catch the vision of what can happen through us when Christ is living on the inside of us by His Holy Spirit.

151

One of the delegates had been praying God would speak to him and bless him through attending the conference. God certainly answered and spoke powerfully into his life. What God said was all the more powerful and effective because never a word was spoken. He arrived at the conference venue in good time and decided to visit the washroom before checking in. As he entered the facility an older man was on his knees washing the floor. In his excitement about attending the conference he simply ignored the man on the floor. You can imagine how he felt when, as he sat in the first plenary session, note book open, pen poised, the first speaker was the toilet cleaner. As he listened he felt greatly humbled. Up till that moment his own preconceived ideas about serving the Lord were all on his own terms. That day he learned an unforgettable lesson about the fundamental principle behind all service in Jesus name - selflessness. There is some truth in the statement that the badge of a servant of Jesus is not a cross but a towel. Jesus, in the full knowledge of who He was in His relationship with His Father, had nothing whatever to prove and was therefore able to pick up a towel, get down on the floor and wash the feet of His disciples including Judas (John 13).

The text we are considering here, 1 Peter 4:11, speaks of serving, *"by the strength which God supplies."* Any service I may perform in my own self-sufficiency will never bring glory to God. Removing self from the picture entirely is what real service in Jesus name is all about. Only then will He be seen and only then will He receive **all** the glory. The word for serve in this verse is the word *diakoneo* (dee-ak-on-eh-o). It means to serve generally. The picture is of a slave waiting at the table. It means having the needs of others as the first concern, being willing to serve in whatever practical way the Lord may indicate. The speaker at the conference obviously saw a need and felt prompted to selflessly meet that need. In so doing he preached his most powerful sermon ever. His primary gifting was probably teaching God's word but the exercise of that gift had greater effectiveness because he had grasped the principle that all service ought to have behind it the same selfless attitude which characterized the Lord Jesus. Other New Testament verses like Romans 12:7

or Ephesians 4:12 which speak of serving use the same route word as that used in 1 Peter 4:11. It is that selfless Christ like attitude which is behind it all.

The wonderfully freeing thing about grasping that principle is that only then will we really prove what serving in God's strength really means. When God "supplies" the strength He does it lavishly. The word is *choregeo* (khor-ayg-eh-o) and it refers to God lavishly supplying what ever we as believers need in serving Him. If you have ever been confronted with something you were sure God wanted you to do but you felt totally inadequate for the task, this concept will fill you with unbounded joy. When Paul talks about realizing his own inadequacy he rejoiced that *"his adequacy is from God"* (2 Cor. 3:5). This word adequacy means ability or competence. Think of it; if I know something is what God wants me to do, He will be my competence. Again we are back to the idea of His indwelling life and Him being all we need. I ask you, how amazing is that? As has been said, "Its the set of the sails, and not the gales, which determines the way we go." My availability to the Lord is all that need concern me.

Challenge

"We have the idea that a man called to the ministry is called to be a different kind of being from other men. According to Jesus Christ, he is called to be the 'doormat' of other men; their spiritual leader but never their superior."[25] See Matthew 20:26-28, *"...whoever wishes to become great among you shall be your servant, and whoever wishes to be first among you shall be your slave; just as the Son of Man did not come to be served, but to serve, and to give His life a ransom for many."* Are you willing to serve your local church in this way?

---

25   Oswald Chambers; *My Utmost for His Highest,* February 23rd

FOURTEEN

There Will Be No Doubt About Why I Am Here

It may be a difficult pill to swallow but in the grand scheme of things you or me being part of a local church really has very little to do with us. Then why bother, you may ask? The final phrase in the section of scripture forming the basis for this book says, *"so that in all things God may be glorified through Jesus Christ, to Whom belongs the glory and dominion for ever and ever. Amen"* (1 Pet. 4:11). Based on his deep experience with Jesus, Peter never lost sight of the grand scheme of things. When Jesus asked His disciples who He was, it was Peter who answered, *"You are the Christ, the Son of the living God"* (Matt. 16:16). Those words are absolutely foundational to everything when it comes to the church. As Jesus Himself said in response to Peter's words, *"...upon this rock I will build My church and the gates of Hades will not overpower it."* What is Jesus doing right now? He is building His church which is part of His coming kingdom but not identical to it. A kingdom is where a king reigns. When Christ is King in our hearts there is part of the kingdom. One day His building of His church will be completed. What a privilege to be part of that unique and vast company of people He has built into His church. A process which began at Pentecost and will be completed the day He returns to call His church to be forever with Himself. The very idea that there is so much controversy about which church, if any, we ought to be part of demonstrates we have completely lost the vision for the bigger picture. The truth of the matter is we don't really believe the Lord's coming is imminent. Nor do we believe that He will one day set up His kingdom here on earth. In fact we don't really believe the Lord is coming again at all. Now, before you protest too loudly allow me to say that if we really did believe in the return of Christ and that we are all going to stand before Him one day, we would be radically different people. There would be no room for denominationalism; no room for the "what do I get out of it" mind set. Neither would there be room for the shallowness caused by the appalling neglect of God's word in today's church. We would be broken hearted over the fact that so many who are lost because they don't know Christ are heading for an eternity without the Lord. Just think of it; when Jesus comes back again and when He sets up His kingdom no one on earth, no one in the heights of Heaven, no one in the awful depths of Hell will be unaware of that event. After all, we are talking about the climax of all the purposes of Almighty God from before time began. Hear again the powerful word of scripture about what was set in motion at the incarnation of Jesus Christ, the Son of God,

> "[He], *although He existed in the form of God, did not regard equality with God a thing to be grasped, but emptied Himself, taking the form of a bond servant, and being made in the likeness of men. Being found in appearance as a man, He humbled Himself by becoming obedient to the point of death, even death on a cross. For this reason also, God highly exalted Him, and bestowed on Him the name which is above every name, so that at the name of Jesus every knee will bow, of those who are in heaven and on earth and under the earth, and that **every tongue will confess that Jesus Christ is Lord to the glory of God the Father**"* (Phil. 2:6-11).

One of the problems we have in giving to God the glory and the praise He rightly deserves is that we have such a limited understanding of who He really is. It is impossible for our finite minds to grasp the vastness of Almighty God. This severe limitation is not helped by the lack of time generally given to quiet and prayerful meditation on God's word. It is there God is able to reveal Himself to us. It is there and there alone where the Holy Spirit is able to expand our minds and our understanding till we are overwhelmed with a deep sense of the greatness of God. For example, think of some of the word pictures given us in scripture.

• He is totally other than we are:

*"Before the mountains were born or You gave birth to the earth and the world, **even from everlasting to everlasting, You are God"** (Ps. 90:2).*

• He is not confined to time and space.

*"Do you not know? Have you not heard? **The everlasting God, the LORD, the creator of the ends of the earth** does not become weary or tired. His understanding is inscrutable"* (Isa. 40:28).

• He is the God of history.

*"...the God of your father, **the God of Abraham, the God of Isaac, the God of Jacob** (Ex. 3:6).*

• He is incomparable.

*"I am the Lord, **and there is no other; besides Me there is no God"** (Isa. 45:5).*

• He is in evidence everywhere.

*"Holy, Holy, Holy, is the LORD of hosts, **the whole earth is full of His glory"** (Isa. 6:3).*

• Because of Who He is no one else deserves the glory.

*"I am the LORD, that is My name, **I will not give My glory to another, nor my praise to graven images"** (Isa. 42:8).*

• He stepped into history.

*"Behold the virgin shall be with child and shall bear a Son, **and they shall call His name Immanuel, which translated means, GOD WITH US"** (Matt. 1:23).*

• What else can we do but worship Him?

*"Blessed be **the God and Father of our Lord Jesus Christ**, Who has blessed us with every spiritual blessing in the heavenly places in Christ...."* (Eph. 1:3).

We could go on highlighting many, many scriptures which demonstrate the greatness and glory of God. But for the purposes of the message of this book we need to see its significance in terms of being part of a local church. Obviously, the local church is part of the universal church. Since all believers, world-wide cannot be together at the same time, the local church is a living, pulsating part of that universal body. Believe it or not but the church is *meant* to be so powerful and so effective in the world, *"so that the manifold wisdom of God might now be made known **through the church** to the rulers and the authorities in the heavenly places"* (Eph. 3:10). We are here, as the church, the people of God, so that together we might demonstrate the existence, reality and power of Almighty God. In one of his New Testament letters John reminds us, *"no one has seen God at any time; if we **love one another, God abides in us,** and His love is perfected in us"* (1 John 4:12). It ought therefore to be fairly obvious and, if I may respectfully say so, deeply challenging, that you or I cannot go it alone. While the life of the living God in the believer is an individual thing, His *"manifold grace"* (1 Pet. 4:10), and His *"manifold wisdom"* (Eph. 3:10) can never be made known by believers on their own. The purpose of God in this church age is to reveal Himself through His people collectively because they are His body, full of His life with that life flowing through each member as He has designed. It is never a matter of individual body parts lying all over the place. You may be a body part with the life of Jesus within you but, you can be sure, you will never function as God intended so long as you remain detached from the rest of the body. The body will only function effectively when it is whole and healthy.

The trouble with today's western church is that we have very little, if any, idea of what it means to have the presence and power of God operating through us as His people. In the days of Elisha the prophet, God gave His servant a supernatural ability to discern what was going on in the enemy camp (2 Kgs. 6). It happened to the extent that the king of Aram thought he had a traitor among his servants. This engendered such anger against Elisha and against God's people that the only recourse the Arameans could think about was murder. Is this ringing any 21st century bells? There are many parts of the world where the only recourse the enemy has against the church is murder and slaughter. The enemies of God's people have nothing to offer that comes anywhere close to what the church has to offer the world through preaching *"Christ crucified"* (1 Cor. 1:23). The devil hates that message with a passion and will stop at nothing to stamp it out. The devil's plan can only operate through devilish methods and that is what we are seeing today.

Going back to Elisha and the Arameans. Eventually they discovered that Elisha was in Dothan so they put their evil plan into action to remove the source of their problem. Being a morning person, Elisha's assistant was up and out for his morning constitutional when he was shocked to find Dothan surrounded by the Aramean army. As far as he was concerned their number was up; they were finished. He, like most of us in the 21st century western church had either completely forgotten, did not know or gave only lip service to a foundational principle, *"those who are with us are more than those who are with them."* The New Testament equivalent is, *"if God is for us, who is against us?"* (Rom. 8:31). Elisha prayed that his assistant's eyes would be opened and, when the Lord opened them *"he saw...the mountain was full of horses and chariots of fire all around Elisha."* In other words he was made aware that all the resources of Heaven are available to the person who trusts God and does things His way. When, oh when will we ever learn to stop aping the world by appointing C.E.O's to run churches or by thinking that if only we had enough money we could do so much more? Any body of believers (local church) that understands that apart from the Lord they are nothing, they have nothing and they can do nothing is poised to become the greatest force for good and for God imaginable. Such a church will be constantly crying out to God because they really believe that apart from Him they can do nothing. Such a church will soon discover that all the resources of Heaven are at their disposal too. What happened to the Arameans next simply knocked Elisha's servant's socks off. God in answer to Elisha's prayer struck the enemy with blindness enabling Elisha to lead them right into the hands of the king of Israel. When everyone involved realized what was going on the king of Israel began to be seen in his true colors. His eagerness is palpable. Unable to contain himself, twice over he said to Elijah, *"shall I kill them? Shall I kill them?"* What happened next must have been a shock to the carnal king of Israel as well as to Elisha's already amazed assistant. God's way was so diametrically opposed to the carnal, worldly way of doing things. To bless those Arameans to the max before sending them home was God's way of handling the situation. This was the very last thing anyone there that day would ever have thought about. The enemies of God's people, Israel, were given a great feast and sent on their way. All the time we insist on a carnal methodology we deny ourselves and our friends outside the church the unimaginable experience of seeing what God can do. The Arameans had been amazingly blessed by the kind of hospitality which originated in God's mind. They had been sent home to their king and to their families (can you imagine the conversation round Aramean dinner tables?). Then we are told, *"the marauding bands of Arameans did not come again into the land of Israel."* If ever there was evidence for God that was it. Elisha must have had a real kick out of the whole episode. His servant, I'm sure, would never be quite the same again. He had just been on a huge learning curve as far as his relationship with God was concerned. As for the Arameans; some would be scratching their heads in disbelief, some may have come to trust Israel's God, some may have wanted to do more. One thing is for sure, all were made aware that the living God was among His people.

Just stop to think for a moment about the anger against evangelical Christians in today's world. Instead of reacting in a carnal way; marching up and down with banners merely demonstrating that we are anti just about everything and, as a result, leaving a thoroughly bad taste in everyone's mouth, we ought to "think Christianly." In other words to get before God to discover His methodology for blessing the gay community, the pro-choice people, people of other faiths etc. What we must rediscover is that when the presence and power of God are among His people things happen that are so obviously of God that all attention is diverted from His people and God alone receives all the glory. This is what a real church looks like and until we get there nothing much is going to change. But when we do get there the real purpose in our being left here on earth is realized, *"in all things God will be glorified through Jesus Christ..."* (1 Pet. 4:11).

A final challenge

If you know Jesus Christ as your personal Saviour and Lord, you are a member of His body the church. As a result you have been given at least one gift which is exactly suited to you and which can only operate effectively within the context of your local church. The proper use of that gift in the power of the Holy Spirit is the only way you will ever bring glory to the Lord and thus be contributing to the realization of the church's purpose in the world. Stop being so self conscious. Stop praying to be sanctified when you already are (1 Cor. 1:2, 30). Stop praying to be filled with the Holy Spirit when not to be is disobedience (Eph. 5:18). Stop working for God. Surrender yourself to Jesus as Lord and allow Him to work in you and through you and all kinds of people will be touched and blessed without you even being aware it is happening (its a good job the Lord does not allow us to know of all the times people are blessed by Him through us). Make it a priority to become part of a local church and selflessly become involved as God has gifted you and have the joy of knowing *"in all things God [is being] glorified through Jesus Christ, to Whom belongs the glory and dominion forever and ever. Amen"*

This is why you need a church.

FIFTEEN

A Final Thought

Some people with whom my wife and I are trying to develop a friendship are, at the moment, very anti-Christian. As far as we can see so far, any mention of anything Christian makes them angry. I suspect one of the reasons for this is that they have very little idea as to what being a Christian means. They probably have some warped idea about religion or people they see as bigots. It is also possible they have had some bad experience with organized religion somewhere along the way. I can't give you hard and fast statistics but I believe it would be true to say that more people have been turned off considering Christianity because of the phony variety, than have been drawn to Christ because of the real thing. It is true to say that this has been the case since day one of the Christian church. Even during the ministry of the great Apostle Paul there was mixed reaction. When he preached the message of the resurrection in Athens, "...*some began to sneer, but others said, 'we shall hear you again concerning this'...But some men joined him and believed...*" (Acts 17:32-34).

It can be immensely frustrating if, every time you try to tell someone what the Lord Jesus means to you, and how He is changing you, you have some phony Christian or church thrown in your face. Now I know that this kind of thing is only an excuse some use to avoid the real issues, but so often there is truth in what they say. It is helpful to keep in mind and be able to tell such people that the existence of a phony only proves the existence of the real thing. You can't have a phony Christian if you don't have a real one with whom to compare him or her. To use an illustration; no one has ever seen a phony $3 bill because there is no such thing as a $3 bill in the first place. It is a well known fact that most people are led to faith in the Lord Jesus

163

because they saw Him in real Christians. How are we going to communicate the good news of the gospel with our pre-Christian friends, and I trust you have some? By new programs in evangelism? Not really, although some of those programs are good and are being used by the Holy Spirit. By your church putting on a big publicity drive? I don't think so. By simply inviting an evangelist in, and expecting him to find and bring in all the sheep who are lost (see Isa. 53:6; John 10:7-11)? No, that is putting the cart before the horse. A preaching evangelist, to use various metaphors, is a reaper or one who draws in the net. His gift is to bring to faith people whose hearts the Holy Spirit has made ready; something He uses the witness of Christians to do. Sometimes evangelists are expected to find and bring in the lost sheep who, at the moment, have no idea they are even lost or that someone cares and is looking for them. Changing the metaphor slightly, there is too much of a chasm at the moment between the people who have the *"abundant"* life which the Good Shepherd talks about in John 10:10 and the ones who are lost and have no hope (see Ephesians 2:12). That means that before any can be brought into the security of knowing Jesus they have to be made aware they are lost and need to be found. For that to happen **we all** have, first of all, to build bridges over the chasm. In other words we need to start to really care and do what ever it takes to build bridges to those who need to see us up close and real. So often the bridges are already there if we but had eyes to see them. What about the people with kids the same age as yours and who go to the same school? Or what about the people who, play golf at the same course as you do, work out in the same gym, collect stamps etc, etc? Those common interests are ready made bridges to enable you to let people see the kind of person you really are. Taking it from there is what will eventually peak their interest. Of course, you are not going to do all this because you see those people as another evangelism project. If you are going to show them you are for real, your love for them will also have to be real. People are not stupid. If my love for my pre-Christian friends is anything other than the real thing, and by that I mean, the very love of Jesus being reproduced in me and through me, then I join the ranks of the phonies.

Jack (not his real name) was a man of the world. He was a together kind of guy; good at his job, a keen golfer and from a decent family. He had it made you would think. However through meeting and getting to know some real Christians he gradually began to see they had something he did not have. He began to ask questions and do some digging around. The day he surrendered his life to the Lord Jesus was a great day for Jack and for his Christian friends. Some of his non-Christian friends raised their eyebrows a bit because they could not understand what got into the guy. Jack was introduced to a local church where he was nurtured in his faith by a group of loving and caring brothers and sisters in Christ. He was baptized and eventually he married a lovely godly woman and is now raising his kids in a godly atmosphere. It is interesting but pretty well the first words out of Jack's mouth when he made his commitment to Christ were, "no one ever told me about this before." What a challenge.

Jill (not her real name either!) came to know Jesus while still quite young. It happened because some Christians took the initiative to creatively reach out to her and others in her community. Because that same group of Christians cared for her and nurtured her in her new life, she too is now baptized, married to a godly man with whom she is raising her family to know and love Jesus too.

Hamish (again not his real name) had met some positive and real Christians. When he fell ill those same Christian friends reached out to him. It soon became evident Hamish was really ill. One of his new friends visited him regularly, each time sharing something from God's word, the Bible, and praying with him. After several visits Hamish and his wife turned their lives over to the Lord Jesus. There was an immediate change. It soon became obvious that Hamish was now filled with a hope he did not have before. Eventually he died. Sad, yes, but not a hopeless sadness. Hamish is now in the presence of the Lord Jesus whom he came to trust as Saviour. He is now, *"absent from the body....and present with the Lord"* (2 Cor. 5:8).

Rob (yet again not his real name) had come under the influence of godly people including his parents. A similar process happened for him which led him to faith in the Lord Jesus and to being cared for among positive Christians. Today he is pastoring a church where his ministry is contributing to the growth of that group of Christians.

All four are real people. I could introduce you to three of them only, for obvious reasons! If you know Jesus then one day I will introduce you to Hamish too!

All this emphasizes the importance of belonging to a local church. Just imagine for a moment that you did everything right and God used you to introduce several people to the Lord Jesus. Wow! Now there's a thought! And, what is even more exciting, it is truly possible. When such a thing happens, what will you do with your new brothers or sisters in Christ? I think you know the answer. You will be looking for a church where they could be nurtured in their new life because they have now become part of Christ's body. The only way that real nurturing can happen is in sharing the life of a healthy group of Christians. I don't mean the granola bar kind of healthy. I mean the *"Christ in you, the hope of glory"* (Col. 1:27) kind of healthy. The work of being real Christians is done outside the church in the real world; the one Jesus talked about in His great prayer in John 17:18; the one into which He sends us to reach the people who are going to believe in Him through our words (John 17:20). The nurturing of those who believe through our word is done in the context of the local church where new Christians are going to experience the richness of belonging to a new family with new brothers and sisters. They will also discover they are now part of a healthy, properly functioning body. It is here it will dawn on them that what is not their's is not something they can keep to themselves. They will very quickly realize they want to be real Christians in the world too so that their friends, who don't understand what is going on will also be introduced to Jesus.

Tell me honestly. Would you be happy to introduce a brand new Christian to the church you attend, if you attend one? Can you be sure that someone who is completely new to the Christian life would be properly nurtured in your church? For many years now it has been my conviction that one of the reasons the Lord does not allow us to see more people coming to know Him is because we are totally unprepared for this to happen. Many are so unprepared that when new Christians do show up, in the full flush of their newly discovered life in Christ, they soon discover that for those in the church, tradition is more important than life. All the traditions and comfort zones are like a huge wet blanket on the new life the new believer has found. How sad is that? Before moving on may I say that the kind of churches which are prepared to welcome new Christians are not always; sometimes, yes, but not always, the kind that are contemporary with the upbeat music etc. I have known churches over the years which are the kind of places that would never be featured in the Christian press or made a fuss of in the large conferences. But they know how to love people and to care for them. When a new Christian shows up they open their hearts and their homes to that person hardly even noticing any of the baggage and trappings of the old life such people may be bringing with them. May I encourage you to think seriously about that.

So, what is missing? The short answer is that the glory of God is no longer in evidence in most churches. Allow me to illustrate. I don't know when you last read through the book of Judges in the Old Testament. If you have not read it for a while I urge you to read it soon. While there are some high spots, it is, generally speaking a very sad catalogue of events. The heady days of Joshua's leadership and the leadership of the generation of *"elders who survived Joshua, and had seen all the great work of the Lord which He had done for Israel"* (Judg. 2:7), were a thing of the past. Now *"there arose another generation after them who did not know the Lord, nor yet the work which He had done for Israel. Then the sons of Israel did evil in the sight of the Lord and served* (or worshipped) *the Baals"* (Judg. 2:10,- 11). From then on there were times of repentance when God would raise up another Judge who would give godly leadership for a time. However with the death of each judge there was further deterioration in the quality of Israel's relationship with God. The quality of the Judges also deteriorated from men like Gideon down to Samson who, although God used him in the end, was far from being all God intended him to be. His selfishness and womanizing was his downfall. Things became so bad that, by the time we come to the end of the book of Judges, we are confronted with the sordid story of unbelievable abuse and, one about a Levite of all people taking a job as a family priest and presiding over the worship of family idols. The book ends with this revealing sentence, *"In those days there was no king in Israel; everyone did what was right in his own eyes"* (Judg. 21:25). You see, 21st century post modernism is as old as the hills!

It is interesting to see that even during this time of deterioration, when the Judges governed Israel, God was doing something beautiful. We are introduced to a delightful young woman called Ruth. From her marriage to Boaz came the line which led, through King David to the manger in Bethlehem where the Son of God was born whose legal but not biological father, was Joseph. This is a reminder that, no matter how bad things may become, God's great plan will never be thwarted.

We then move into the books of Samuel. From before his birth Samuel was dedicated to the Lord. He learned to serve God even as a boy under Eli. However, there came a time when God called him and, because Samuel responded obediently, God raised him up to be a prophet to His people Israel. All the time Samuel was growing up the spiritual and moral deterioration in Israel continued. Eli's sons were supposed to be in the service of God in the temple but, for them it was only a job and, in no sense a calling. They were immoral, greedy and selfish. There father, Eli, although he knew all that was going on, as did most other people, he did nothing to preserve the honor of the Lord's name. Things were at an all time low. *"Word from the Lord was rare in those days…"* (1 Sam. 3:1). There is nothing more sad than the people of God, and I include 21st century churches in that category, going through the motions and not ever realizing how serious things have become. There are regular services but we know and so does the outside world that all kinds of immorality and sin is going on, only to be swept under the rug.

Hearing a real word from God is "rare." As with Israel, so with us, the enemy is having a field day.

Israel remembered their history but learned nothing from it. When the enemy came against them they thought all they had to do was to produce the ark of God. Please try to grasp the significance of what was happening. They brought out the ark of God. This was the same ark which Moses had made at God's instructions and placed in the Holy of Holies in the tabernacle in the desert. When that event happened (See Ex. 40), *"the glory of the Lord filled the Tabernacle."* So awesome was that moment that Moses was no longer able to enter the tabernacle. From then on only the High Priest could go into the Holy of Holies and that only once a year on the Day of Atonement and not without the blood of the sacrifice. Tradition has it that he had a cord tied around his waste so that, if he became overwhelmed with the glory of God he could be pulled out. No one else dared to enter. Now we come to the early days of Samuel. Israel is confronted with her enemies. Thinking to take this same ark all the time taking it for granted that because the ark was there the presence and power of God was there. The tragic irony of the situation is powerfully obvious on reading 1 Samuel 4:4, *"So the people sent to Shiloh, and from there they carried the ark of the covenant of the LORD of hosts who sits above the cherubim;* **and the two sons of Eli,** *Hophni and Phinehas,* **were there with the ark of the covenant of God."** In other words the whole thing was a complete mockery. The people of God had descended to the level of superstition. By the time we get to the end of chapter 4 of 1 Samuel the real heart of Israel's problems is revealed. Israel is defeated by the enemy and the ark of God has been captured. The sons of Eli died in the battle and that, together with the deeply shocking news of the capture of the ark of God brought on Eli's death. His pregnant daughter in law, the wife of Phinehas is so shocked, not only at the death of her husband but also at the news of the capture of the ark of the covenant that she gives birth to her son. In naming the boy she sums up the whole situation and shows more spiritual discernment than all the so called leaders of Israel, who ought to have known better. *"She called the boy Ichabod* *saying,* **the glory has departed from Israel, for the ark of God was taken**" (1 Sam. 4:21-22). Read on into 1 Samuel chapter five and you will see that, although Israel was defeated, God remained totally sovereign and all powerful.

It breaks my heart every time I pass a building which was once a church but is now a Thrift Shop, an electrical store or someone's home. On one such building some discerning soul had pasted a notice which read, "AN ENEMY HAS DONE THIS." Yet, I sometimes feel that, perhaps even worse is a church which is still going through the motions; where there are services every Sunday, but no one, other than the membership, ever pays any attention to the place. Its just the place where some religious people go. Its really totally irrelevant in the minds of most people. In other words *"THE GLORY HAS DEPARTED."*

As was the case for ancient Israel, so is the case for our 21st century church, God is still God. Today's church has the added advantage that Christ, who rose from the dead is still alive. He is still fulfilling the promise He made when He said, *"I will build my church; and the gates of Hades will not overpower it"* (Matt. 16:18). God's purposes will be fulfilled but unless something happens in today's church there is so much that will be missed. God raised up Samuel. He was just a boy when God began using him. Later in his life God did great things through him and the ark of God and all it signified came back to Israel. Israel humbled themselves before God, they dealt with their sin and were restored to a right relationship with the Lord. Gone was the immorality, idolatry and superstition. The same old enemy came against them but, this time, the glory of God was among them again and, *"the Lord thundered with a great thunder on that day against the Philistines and confused them, so that they were routed before Israel."* Read 1 Samuel chapter 7. The difference when the glory of God is among His people is that things happen which can only be attributed to God and He receives all the praise. This is how it ought to be because He alone is worthy of such praise.

Not until we have genuine revival will anything in today's church really change for the better. What is the main characteristic of genuine revival among God's people? It is that the **THE GLORY OF GOD IS THERE.** That will never happen until, under the power of the Holy Spirit we are broken over the sin, immorality and deadness that has afflicted us and the very breath of God sweeps through the people of God. When the glory of God is among the people of God, everyone is aware of it. There is, quite simply, an overwhelming reverence and a deep routed awareness of the Almighty.

It is my heart-felt prayer that every reader of this book will be deeply touched by the Holy Spirit to the extent that there will be created in all our hearts an insatiable hunger for the Glory of God to come. Even as I typed the last sentence the Holy Spirit brought the words of the late Bessie P. Head to mind. The tears of longing and joyous anticipation are flowing even as I think of what it would be like.

O Breath of life, come sweeping through us,
Revive Thy church with life and power;
O Breath of life, come, cleanse, renew us,
And fit Thy church to meet this hour.
O Wind of God, come bend us, break us,
Till humbly we confess our need;
Then in Thy tenderness remake us,
Revive, restore, for this we plead.
O Breath of love, come breathe within us,
Renewing thought and will and heart;
Come, Love of Christ, afresh to win us,
Revive Thy church in every part.
O Heart of Christ, once broken for us,
'Tis there we find our strength and rest;
Our broken, contrite hearts now solace,
And let Thy waiting church be blest.
Revive us, Lord! Is zeal abating

While harvest fields are vast and white?

Revive, us Lord, the world is waiting,

Equip Thy church to spread the light.

—Bessie P. Head

One more challenge

Ask God to make you willing for genuine revival to touch you personally and to spread to every church in your community (see top of page 97 and also the Introduction, paragraph 2).

Also by Clayton Dougan and companion to *So Why Do I Need A Church*:
So Why Do I Need THE BIBLE?

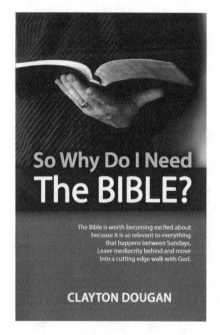

Years ago, Clayton's marriage almost fell apart, mainly because his ministry as an evangelist became all consuming. There was little time for a relationship with God or with his wife. He was a busy preacher, but was cold as ice in his heart. It was one of the blackest times of his life. then the Holy Spirit brought him to a place of utter brokenness and deep repentance. He discovered the simple fact of Jesus living inside him and that all here is in God was his to enjoy...What did Clayton learn because of his difficult time? Read the Bible consistently...God's Word spoke to specific situations in his life at just the right time. He received peace in troubled times and a direction in confusing times. It brought healing to His marriage and family.

The enemy, Satan, does not give up easily. His constant strategy is to keep you from enjoying the peace and confidence of walking with God. Without doubt, keeping you from the prayerful, meditative, and obedient study of God's word is the only way you can grow in your union with Christ. Through planned strategy the enemy comes against God's people (2 Cor.2:11; Eph.6:11).

In this book Clayton Dougan shares illustrations from personal experience to relate the book to real living. He shows how developing good and godly habits is well within the grasp of the busiest reader and makes it clear where to find the added help.

ISBN: 9781926765044
132 pages